THE GERMAN ARMY
MOUNTAIN SOLDIER
OF WORLD WAR II

Wade Krawczyk & Bart Jansen

THE GERMAN ARMY
MOUNTAIN SOLDIER
OF WORLD WAR II

Wade Krawczyk & Bart Jansen

The Crowood Press

First published in 2009 by
The Crowood Press Ltd
Ramsbury, Marlborough
Wiltshire SN8 2HR

www.crowood.com

British Library Cataloguing-in-Publication Data
A catalogue record for this book is available from the British Library.

ISBN 978 1 84797 097 8

Acknowledgements
Wade would like to thank firstly his wife Melissa and son Max for their
patient and unflagging support while he was working on this book. Many
thanks also to those listed below, who gave freely of their knowledge,
their time and their wonderful collections in order for us to bring this
aspect of military history to life. This book hopefully reflects your
generosity.
   Bart wishes to thank his wife Annemieke and their two daughters
Angela and Jolanda for their patience and understanding. Special thanks
go to Walter Waldegger for sharing his memories and his knowledge of
Gebirgsjäger equipment. Invaluable knowledge has also been shared
by fellow Gebirgsjäger collectors whom Bart has had the pleasure of
knowing for many years. Anyone wanting to contact Bart on Wehrmacht
Gebirgsjäger issues can do so on *GJR136@gmail.com.*

Edited by Martin Windrow
Typeset by Carolyn Griffiths, Cambridge
Printed and bound in India by Replika Press

CONTENTS

INTRODUCTION

When the German Wehrmacht comprising the three new national armed services was created in March 1935, to replace the small Reichswehr that had been subject to the restrictions of the Treaty of Versailles since March 1919, it heralded a period of unprecedented change and modernization. Those limitations had been keenly felt in a country that remembered the first harsh years following defeat at the end of World War I – years of occupation by Allied troops, armed insurrections in German cities and semi-official warfare on the eastern and northern borders. The leaders of the Reichswehr had made clandestine efforts to evade the full effects of the Versailles limits, and it had long been accepted among German strategists and tacticians that the shape, doctrine and methods of the former armed services had to be adapted for a new kind of warfare.

Now allowed to expand rapidly through the introduction of universal conscription, the three services (*Heer, Kriegsmarine* and *Luftwaffe*) were able to devote a good deal of Germany's resources, both material and intellectual, to the building of modern armed forces. For the Army this meant, notably, the creation of mechanized and armoured formations, reflecting a determination to achieve flexibility and mobility in order to prevent a repeat of the positional war of attrition that had nailed the Kaiser's armies down on the stagnant Western Front of 1915–18. However, amid all this change there were still some aspects of the Army that required an approach more tested and proven over time.

One of these 'traditional' branches of warfare was the use of mountain light infantry or *Gebirgsjäger*. These troops were required to take the fight to the enemy – and to prevail – in mountainous and inhospitable terrain, no matter what the weather conditions. The experience of mountain fighting in World War I, particularly on the Italian front alongside Austrian troops, was still fresh in the memory (it was, after all, the type of combat in which a young officer named Erwin Rommel had first distinguished himself). In the frustrating and unforgiving environment of the mountains, mechanization had little to contribute; indeed, hardly any of the new technology could make a real difference to the essentials of warfare in the mountains, which still demanded extremely hardy troops trained in special skills. While their job could be made easier by the provision of better equipment, weapons and communications, the basic demands and tools of the Gebirgsjäger's trade necessarily remained unchanged.

The most basic task of all – simply moving troops and their equipment and supplies to where they were needed – was enormously challenging in mountain terrain. Beyond the end of the paved roads wheeled transport was impossible, and even tracked vehicles like the handy little Kettenkrad motorcycle-halftrack could not get up the steepest, narrowest tracks. The traditional skills of working with pack-mules and ponies were still vital (indeed, the Mountain Troops would also have to teach themselves how to handle dogsleds, reindeer and Bactrian camels when serving on the far northern and southern flanks of the Eastern Front). The engineers of Gebirgs Pioniere units had to blast through rockfalls, create paths above dizzying drops and rig rope bridges across raging torrents. Radio communications were always precarious in the mountains, and Gebirgs Nachrichten signallers had to be adept at rigging long aerials in treetops and placing chains of relay stations. The medics of the Gebirgs Sanitäts Kompanien had to deal with frostbite as well as gunshot wounds, and to master the delicate skills of evacuating casualties with ropes and special stretchers.

Units of the Reichswehr drawn from men born and raised in the south of Germany, who were accustomed since childhood to life in the mountains, had kept the core skills alive, as had the Bavarian State Police. With the birth of the Wehrmacht these men were gathered under an officer named Ludwig Kübler; within two years the first regiment had grown into a brigade, and in April 1938 into 1. Gebirgs Division. The simultaneous annexation of Austria and absorption of her army brought a new influx of mountain-bred men, and second to fifth divisions were quickly formed, to be followed by others during wartime.

The Gebirgsjäger, Gebirgsartillerie, Gebirgspioniere and their support and service troops fought in terrain as diverse as the snowbound arctic forests of Finland, the towering Caucasus Mountains in the far south of the Soviet Union, the Italian Alps and the mountains of the Balkans, the baking hills of the Mediterranean, and even – in a few cases – in the desert of North Africa. In these testing landscapes they met the challenges presented to them by the terrain and the enemy alike, and fought with a skill that brought them credit and respect. Their presence in such battles as Narvik (1940) and Crete (1941) proved decisive and helped ensure German victories.

In this book the authors present a range of the uniforms and specialized equipment used by the Mountain Light Infantry and supporting arms of the German Army Mountain Troops in World War II, together with examples of awards presented to these troops. While the focus of this book is on the Army, the unique equipment and uniform items were also used by other German mountain warfare troops such as units of the Waffen-SS, Mountain Police and Customs personnel. These soldiers were all part of the brotherhood who wore the Edelweiss on their caps.

Collectively, we wish to thank the following individuals for their assistance and time in making this work possible: Karl Baldauf, Anton Breuker, Jason Burmeister, Mario Kabalt, Peter v Lukacs, Simon Orchard, Daniël Paap, Karl Ploner, Marco Plötz, Siegfried Schuchter, Ludwig Thoma, Walter Waldegger, Marjolijn Veendorp, Pieter Verbruggen, Tommy Vervest, Daan Vonk, and lastly Phil (the dog) and Winston (the Haflinger).

The Mountain Divisions

While this book is concerned with uniforms, it may be helpful to readers to have a basic order-of-battle of these formations with the numbered designations of their constituent 'teeth' units, though not their service troops. The briefest summaries of their theatres of operations may also be of some interest.

1. Gebirgs Division

Gebirgsjäger Regimenter 98 & 99 (& 100, until 1940), Gebirgs Artillerie Rgt 79, Panzerjäger Abeilung 54 (anti-tank battalion), *Gebirgs Pionier Abteilung 54* (engineer battalion), *Gebirgs Nachrichten Abteilung 54* (signals battalion)
Depot: Garmisch, Bavaria, in military region *Wehrkreis VII* (mixed German and Austrian personnel)
Commanding generals: Generalmajor Ludwig Kübler (1938–41), GenMaj Hubert Lanz (1942–43), GenMaj Hermann Kress (1943), Generalleutnant Walter Stettner, Ritter von Grabenhofen (1943–44), GenLt Josef Kubler (1945)
Served: Poland (1939), France & Low Countries (1940), Yugoslavia (1941), southern USSR (June 1941–March 1943), Greece & Yugoslavia (1943–44), Hungary & Austria (1944–45 – briefly retitled 1. Volks Gebirgs Division)

2. Gebirgs Division

Gebirgsjäger Rgt 136 & 137, Gebirgs Artillerie Rgt 111, Radfahrer Abt 67 (motorcycle battalion), *Gebirgs Panzerjäger Abt 47, Gebirgs Pionier Abt 82, Gebirgs Nachrichten Abt 67*
Depot: Innsbruck, Austria, *Wehrkreis XVIII* (Austrian personnel)
Commanding generals: GenLt Valentin Feuerstein (1938–41), GenMaj Ernst Schlemmer (1941–42), GenLt Georg, Ritter von Hengl (1942–43), GenMaj Hans Degan (1944–45)
Served: Poland (1939), Norway (1940–41), northern USSR & Finland (June 1941–late 1944), Western Front & southern Germany (February–May 1945)

3. Gebirgs Division

Gebirgsjäger Rgt 138 & 139, Gebirgs Artillerie Rgt 112, Radfahr Abt 68, Gebirgs Panzerjäger Abt 48, Gebirgs Pionier Abt 83, Gebirgs Nachrichten Abt 68
Depot: Graz, Austria, *Wehrkreis XVIII* (German personnel)
Commanding generals: GenLt Eduard Dietl (1938–40), GenLt Hans Kreysing (1940–43), GenMaj Egbert Picker (1943), GenLt August Wittmann (1943–44), GenLt Paul Klatt (1944–45)
Served: Poland (1939), Norway (1940), northern USSR and Finland (June 1941–autumn 1942), southern USSR (1942–44), Romania, Hungary & Czechoslovakia (1944–45), some elements Lapland and Norway

4. Gebirgs Division

Gebirgsjäger Rgt 13 & 91, Gebirgs Artillerie Rgt 94, Radfahr Abt 94, Gebirgs Panzerjäger Abt 94, Gebirgs Pionier Abt 94, Gebirgs Nachrichten Abt 94
Depot: Dresden, Saxony, *Wehrkreis IV* (mixed German and Austrian personnel)
Commanding generals: GenLt Karl Eglseer (1940–42), GenLt Hermann Kress (1943), GenLt Julius Braun (1944), GenLt Friedrich Breith (1944–45)
Served: Yugoslavia & Greece (1941), southern USSR (June 1941–late 1944), Hungary, Czechoslovakia & Austria (1944–45)

5. Gebirgs Division

Gebirgsjäger Rgt 85 & 100, Gebirgs Artillerie Rgt 95, Radfahr Abt 95, Gebirgs Panzerjäger Abt 95, Gebirgs Pionier Abt 95, Gebirgs Nachrichten Abt 95
Depot: Salzburg, Austria, *Wehrkreis XVIII* (mixed German and Austrian personnel)
Commanding generals: GenLt Julius Ringel (1940–44), GenMaj Max-Gunther Schrank (1945)
Served: Greece (1941), Crete (May–September 1941), Norway (1941–42), northern USSR (January 1942–December 1943), Italy (January 1944–April 1945)

6. Gebirgs Division

Gebirgsjäger Rgt 141 & 143, Gebirgs Artillerie Rgt 118, Gebirgs Kraftrad Abt 157 (motorcycle battalion), *Gebirgs Panzerjäger Abt 157, Gebirgs Pionier Abt 91, Gebirgs Nachrichten Abt 96*
Depot area: Klagenfurt, Austria, *Wehrkreis XVIII* (German personnel)
Commanding generals: GenMaj Ferdinand Schörner (1940–42), GenLt Philipp Christian (1942–44), GenMaj Max Pemsel (1944–45)
Served: Greece (1941 – some elements also Crete), Norway (September 1941), northern USSR & Finland (October 1941–late 1944), Norway (1945)

7. Gebirgs Division

Gebirgsjäger Rgt 144 & 206, Gebirgs Artillerie Rgt 82, Kraftrad Abt 99, Gebirgs Panzerjäger Abt 99, Gebirgs Pionier Abt 99, Gebirgs Nachrichten Abt 99
Depot: Nuremberg, Bavaria, *Wehrkreis XIII*
(Re-formed from 99. Jäger Division, winter 1941/42)
Commanding general: GenLt August Krakau
Served: Finland (spring 1942–late 1944), Norway (1944–45)

8. Gebirgs Division

Gebirgsjäger Rgt 142 & 144, Gebirgs Artillerie Rgt 124, plus unidentified divisional units
Depot: Norway, but dependent on *Wehrkreis XVIII*
Commanding general: unidentified
Believed formed Norway (1942), perhaps never to full strength; served northern USSR & Finland; Italy (late 1944–April 1945)

9. Gebirgs Division

Depot: Dachstein, Austria, *Wehrkreis XVII*
Designation allocated to two small battlegroups successively:
Kampfgruppe Krautler/ Gebirgsjäger Rgt 139 (Norway, 1945)
Kampfgruppe Semmering/ Gebirgsjäger Rgt 140 (Austria, 1945)

188. Gebirgs Division

(1943) *Reserve Gebirgsjäger Rgt 136, 137 & 139, I Bataillon/ Reserve Gebirgs Artillerie Rgt 112, Reserve Gebirgs Pionier Abt 83 (?)*
Depot: Salzburg, Austria, *Wehrkreis XVIII*
Commanding general: GenLt Wilhelm von Hösslin (1943–45)
Formed from training and replacement units as 188. Reserve Gebirgs Division in Italy (autumn 1943); redesignated as full Gebirgs Division in Croatia (late 1944); served in Balkans (1945)

(**Opposite**) The SdKfz 2 Kettenkraftrad 'motorcycle-halftrack', which first saw action on Crete in May 1941. Its 36bhp engine and unique method of traction allowed the 'Kettenkrad' to tow loads of up to 4 tons on level ground, including guns of up to 7.5cm calibre. The 10.5cm M40 Gebirgshaubitze of the mountain artillery regiments' heavy battery broke down into four sub-assemblies for towing by Kettenkrads.

HEADGEAR

Officer's service cap (Schirmmütze)

The peaked service cap for officers had been worn in various forms during the inter-war years. Prior to the Third Reich period (starting in 1933) the cap worn by the Reichswehr had a distinctly flat crown of so-called *Tellerform* (literally 'plate form'); caps of later manufacture increasingly adopted the more pleasing *Sattelform* ('saddle form') with a more sweeping outline. From 1935 the insignia consisted of the national emblem *(Hoheitszeichen)* of the new Nazi Germany (an eagle with outstretched wings, clutching a wreathed Nazi Party swastika), surmounting a stamped metal wreath

with a central raised metal cockade in the national colours of black, white and red. In late 1935 this was superseded by a wreath with a more raised profile, and a new eagle with wings further outstretched, which was to be duplicated on the right breast of the tunic. The insignia could also be obtained at the officer's expense in bullion embroidered form. (Note that throughout this book references to insignia made in 'silver' and 'bullion' should be understood to mean aluminium.)

(Left) All Army officers were required to purchase the *Schirmmütze*. The cloth and colour of the 'pavilion' (crown) were of varying quality. The basic cloth was tricot, but finer-grade wool fabrics like *Döskin* were available to those with the money. The capband was made of dark green badgecloth. The crown and both edges of the band displayed piping in the wearer's Waffenfarbe or branch-of-service colour; for the Gebirgsjäger this was light green or *hellgrün*. Officers wore a silver braided double cord chinstrap, secured by silver pebbled-finish buttons.

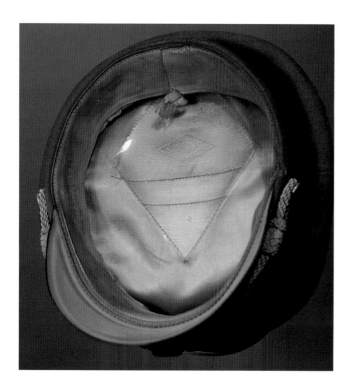

(Left) This example is from the prestigious firm of Robert Lubstein, better know by its acronym 'Erel' (from the initials 'R.L'). This maker's mark is visible both on the sweatband and behind the celluloid sweatshield, a feature of this particular firm. The retailer, a Vienna company, is also included in the marking. The cap is marked *'Sonderklasse'*, meaning 'special quality'. Note that the underside of the peak matches the colour of the silk lining, an almost universal feature of these peaked caps.

(Above right) This particular cap displays a not uncommon mixture of both stamped metal and bullion embroidered insignia. Note between the two universal elements the stemless edelweiss tradition badge, which from May 1939 was permitted for wear by serving mountain troops. This badge is of two-piece construction, with two fixing prongs on the rear surface.

Enlisted ranks' service cap

The peaked service cap for enlisted and non-commissioned personnel was in the same general style as the officer's cap, but usually of a simpler quality, and featured a black leather chinstrap instead of bullion cords. This example displays the typical retention of the early 'plate-shaped' crown, and is manufactured from a basic ribbed twill cloth. The badges are all of stamped aluminium; embroidered badges were only permitted on private-purchase caps. The leather chinstrap is secured with two plain black buttons and passes through two black metal tightening buckles and end loops. This example has some age crazing to the patent leather finish.

(Below) The interior is typical of these enlisted-grade caps; it has a plain orange waterproof cloth lining, and an unmarked celluloid sweatshield.

(Bottom) The rear of the sweatband is marked with the unit, in this case 13 Kompanie/ Gebirgsjäger Regiment 137/ III Bataillon. These enlisted caps were generally issued to troops at the depot, and then handed back in when they left for their assignments.

(Above right) The standard issue aluminium national emblem and wreathed cockade badges, with the mountain troops' edelweiss tradition badge pinned between. Note the colour of the light green Waffenfarbe, which can vary markedly from item to item; a wide range of exact shades will be found on many surviving examples of caps and tunics.

Officer's 'old style' field cap *(Knautschmütze)*

A field cap for officers was introduced in 1934, and was popularly referred to as the *Knautschmütze* or 'crumple cap' for its ability to be folded and placed in the pocket or baggage. When the officer's sidecap-style field cap was introduced in 1935 the previous pattern was designated the *Feldmütze alter Art* or 'old style field cap' to indicate that it

had been superseded. Officially officers who had bought them were only to use the 'crumple caps' until 1942; however, they proved extremely popular with officers who possessed them, and examples could be seen in use by anyone from lieutenants to generals right up to the end of the war.

(**Right**) The cap was of the same basic shape and design as the Schirmmütze, but lacked any stiffening to retain the shape of the crown or capband. This gave it a soft, 'crushed' look – and lent its wearer the desirable appearance of being a front-line veteran. It had no chinstrap or cords, and the peak was made of soft, flexible leather, which allowed the cap to be folded; some examples exist with peaks made of a pressed cardboard material. Others still may be found with peaks of non-flexible *Vulkanfibre*, thus imitating the style of the cap but not actually allowing it to fold.

(**Below**) The interior of this cap is marked to the maker of Joh Seitz of Landau Pfalz.

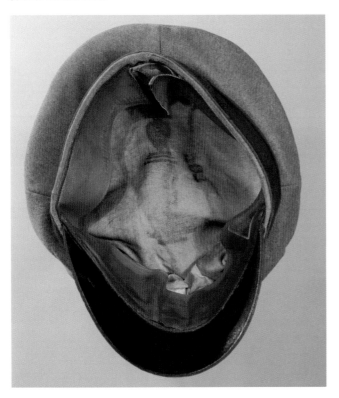

(**Right**) The insignia consisted of the usual national eagle, above a silver wreath and tricolour cockade, both elements being in the flat machine-woven style known as 'BeVo weave' after the abbreviation for Bandfabrik Ewald Vorsteher, the Wuppertal company that was the largest manufacturer of such cloth insignia. (Indeed, the term has come to be generally used for all such flat-woven insignia, even if not produced in Wuppertal.) Early examples of the wreath and cockade, like this one, have a brown-grey base cloth, while the more common later examples have a dark green base. As this example shows, it was common for the two styles to appear together on the same cap. Some very early examples have a wreath that is slightly raised and woven in white cotton, with a metal cockade in the centre.

General officer's mountain cap *(Bergmütze)*

On occasions an item of uniform can become iconic, and is associated with a particular branch of the military; the item most identified with the Gebirgsjäger was the mountain cap or *Bergmütze*. Similar to that worn by mountain troops in World War I, this headgear was worn in preference to all others and, with the edelweiss badge on the left side, it became the proud mark of the mountain soldier. Popular and functional, it eventually provided the model for the design of the universal field cap for German servicemen, the 1943 *Einheitsfeldmütze*. The outer folded flap could be pulled down to protect the lower part of the face (something not often done in practice), and was secured by two front buttons. The front peak or visor of the original *Bergmütze* was shorter than that of the later M43 cap.

(**Below**) This particular *Bergmütze* is for a general officer; since such caps were privately ordered from tailors many variations existed, and this example is made of a light grey *Döskin*, a relatively expensive carded wool fabric. The crown piping was sewn in at the time of manufacture, dating this example to after October 1942, when officers were first required to affix metallic piping (silver, but gold for general officers). Note also the general's gold-finished pebbled buttons.

(**Above**) The silver BeVo machine-woven eagle and tricolour cockade on a 'T'-shaped backing, machine-sewn to the cap at the time of manufacture.

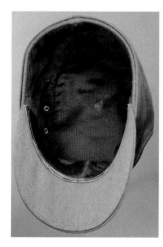

(**Left**) The lining was usually a grey drill or tricot fabric, and after 1938 caps were required to have one or two ventilation eyelets high on each side. The lining of this cap is of brown artificial silk, with a leather sweatband at the forehead area. The cloth-covered visor is made of soft leather or fibreboard.

(**Right**) The edelweiss tradition badge for all branches and ranks of the Gebirgstruppe was introduced in May 1939. This example is quite typical, except for an added dark green badgecloth backing – a private touch sometimes seen on the caps of all ranks.

Officer's *Bergmütze*

This is an early example, since the metallic crown piping of officer's rank is absent. Prior to its introduction in October 1942 the only things that set officers' mountain caps apart from those of their men were the quality of the materials and the use of silver-coloured wire in the machine-woven eagle badge. Fabrics used for caps varied depending on the buyer's budget. Officers' uniform items were purchased with vouchers *(Uniformbezugschein)*, which could be used either at the outlets of the *Offizier Kleiderkasse* (literally 'officer's clothing fund') or at authorized private tailors. This cap is made from a quality light grey brushed wool.

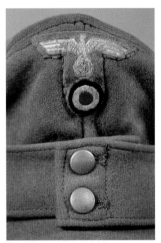

(**Above**) The use of silver metallic thread for the BeVo-woven eagle indicates officer status. The 'T'-shaped badge is the early type woven on an 'earth-brown' backing, and like many early examples it is hand-sewn to the cap. Note the silver-finish 12mm pebbled-texture buttons for the front flap closure.

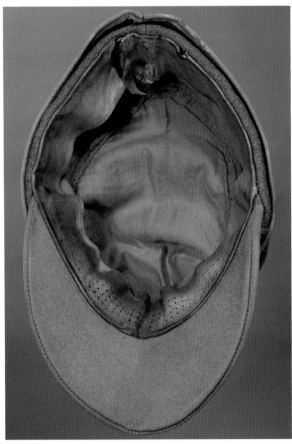

Officer's *Bergmütze*

If the officer had the means he could spend extra on his uniform from his own pocket; quality thus varied from the standard to the highly fashionable, but the general appearance of the standard item had to be maintained. The example shown here is made of a medium-quality brushed wool in light grey-green, a shade usually associated with earlier caps. This is confirmed by the fact that, in accordance with the October 1942 order, officers' metallic crown piping has been retro-fitted; a thin bullion cord has been faultlessly hand-sewn around the crown seam. This particular cap is otherwise conventional; note that like the example opposite, it lacks ventilation eyelets high in the sides of the crown.

Here the 'T'-shaped one piece machine-woven badge is worked on the later dark green base cloth. Note that the silver-coloured (aluminium) thread has also been used for the 'white' ring of the cockade, as well as for the national emblem above. The silver crown piping has been expertly attached.

(Right) The interior of the cap above is lined with a hard-wearing brown cotton twill, with a sweatband of a composite leatherette material which has broken down with age and wear. Note around the edge of the crown the visible white stitching, showing where the officer's piping was added in 1942.

(Left) A Leutnant of Gebirgs-jäger wearing the *Bergmütze* in the field. Note also the *Windjacke* (*see* pages 90–91).

(Far left) The interior of the cap on page 12 reveals a good quality lining made from a grey tricot drill fabric. The superior sweatband was originally a buff colour but has darkened with wear; it has a small bow of ribbon at the rear join, a sign of private tailoring. Note the perforations at the forehead area to help with ventilation.

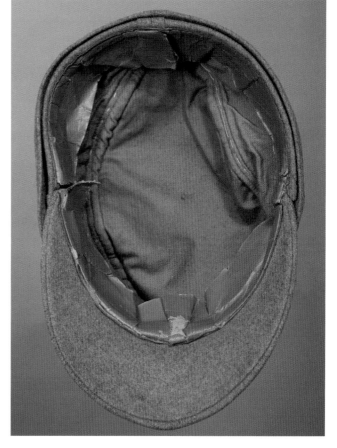

Officer's *Bergmütze*

In comparison with previous examples this is a much more humble item. It outwardly resembles the enlisted ranks' issue cap, but is actually tailored. As the war went on, raw materials

(Bottom) The lining is of brown cotton tricot, stamped with the maker's name – Hermann Gollhofer of Anichstr.5, Innsbruck. The sweatband seems to have been fitted later in the war, and has a lace threaded through it – a feature of some Austrian-made caps; it is impressed with the name Carl Bremer of Nordhorn.

of all kinds became scarce, and even private-purchase items tended towards a poorer appearance. The fabric used here is a lower quality green-grey wool, and the cap is cut with a low profile. There is a single ventilation eyelet on each side finished in field-grey paint. Even the buttonholes on the turn-down flap have been rather simply hand-sewn. It has the post-1942 officer piping, but aluminium bullion thread is replaced by white twist cord, applied by hand; such expedients were common late in the war.

(Below) The insignia are interesting in that the wearer has created his own in place of the usual 'T'-type; they are both rather crudely hand-sewn in place. The eagle seems to be that used on the officers' sidecap, and the separate cockade is for an enlisted ranks' cap, with the diamond-shaped backing folded under and sewn down.

(Bottom) The standard edelweiss badge has a nice detail: the remains of a real flower tucked behind it. Photos reveal that soldiers sometimes wore the symbolic mountain flower (or even a feather) on their caps, perhaps as a good luck charm.

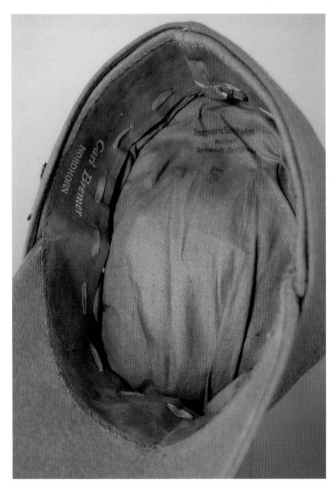

Officer's *Bergmütze*

Another later-war cap, showing hints of shortcuts in the construction. The standard of mountain troop clothing seems to have remained fairly high, obviously in consideration of the harsh environments in which the Gebirgstruppe had to operate; but after the introduction of the very similar universal field cap in mid 1943 production of the issue *Bergmütze* ceased. However, officers continued to have caps tailored to this pattern. Although this example is a tailored item it closely resembles the earlier enlisted ranks' issue. The wool is of an ordinary grade, and ventilation eyelets have been omitted. Post-October 1942 officer's piping was fitted during construction.

(Below) The lining (which again bears the mark of Hermann Gollhofer of Innsbruck) is of common off-white tricot, and the sweatband is a crescent-shape of cheap leatherette above the forehead only.

(Below) The front badge is interesting. This BeVo machine-woven insignia is made to be used as a 'T'- shape, but the base cloth (in last-pattern grey colour) has simply been folded into a triangle and machine-sewn in place with zig-zag stitches during construction of the cap. This may have been done to speed up production, or may reflect the use of semi-skilled labour.

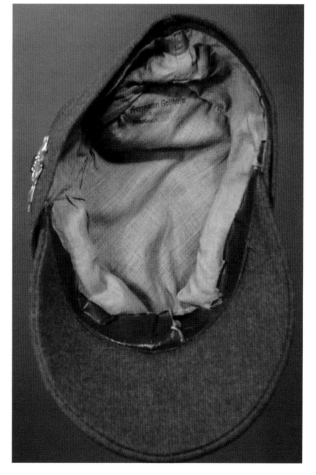

Enlisted ranks' *Bergmütze*

This is an example of an early enlisted ranks' *Bergmütze*. The high shape, short peak and wide turn-down flap make the cap reminiscent of the World War I period Austrian mountain troops' cap, which had a more 'pillbox' shape. The cloth is a strong field-green wool, with a fairly stiff peak. The crown of this particular cap has been personalized by the wearer with a safety pin – still inside – to pinch the front of the crown together, giving a more 'rakish' shape. There is a single ventilation eyelet at each side, finished in *feldgrau* paint. In place of 13mm pebbled-texture silver buttons the turn-down flap is secured by two brown buttons of the material known as *'Steinnuss'* (literally, 'stone nut'), made from the corozo nut.

(**Right**) From this angle the deep section of the edelweiss tradition badge can be seen. It is sewn on using five small fixing holes, four around the petals of the flower and one at the base of the stem. The badge is made in two pieces: the base flower with the stem was stamped from zinc or aluminium, and a gold-finished bunch of stamens was then fixed to the centre.

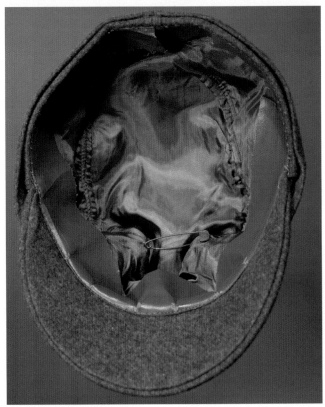

(**Above**) The enlisted version of the 'T'-form insignia is machine-woven in grey thread on a dark green base. The previous pattern had a white eagle on dark green; the next, and final pattern had a grey eagle on grey backing. The badge has been hand-sewn to the cap, a method commonly seen especially on early caps. Note the 'woodgrain' pattern of the *Steinnuss* buttons.

(**Above**) The lining is a grey artificial silk, also commonly used for tunic linings. The orange-brown leatherette sweatband extends all the way round the cap. Note the period safety-pin used to crimp the front of the crown into the desired shape.

Enlisted ranks' *Bergmütze*

The example seen here is the classic enlisted-pattern *Bergmütze*, seen on many fronts and worn as long as the cap held together. This headgear was greatly prized as the symbol of an elite group of soldiers; before mid-1943 its design was unique in the ranks of the Army, since almost all other troops wore the boat-shaped *Feldmütze* (the 'Schiffchen'). The *Gebirgsjäger* was immediately recognizable, and his cap set him apart as something special. It was also popular for its practicality: it sat on the head more securely and warmly than a sidecap, its peak gave shade from the sun and the glare of snow as well as protection from rain, and in extreme weather its flap could be turned down to cover the neck, cheeks and chin.

(Left) Made from a hard-wearing *feldgrau* wool, this cap has an almost 'pillbox' shape from this angle, due to an internal pad to keep the front of the crown standing stiffly upwards. Later caps lacked this feature, and were softer in shape. There is a single ventilation eyelet each side; the peak is of cloth-covered leather; and these pebbled-finish metal buttons are probably later replacements for original brown *Steinnuss* type.

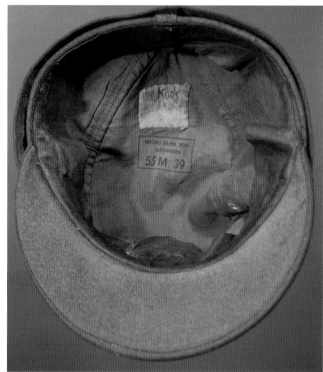

(Above) This cap has a sturdy brown cotton lining, and a full sweatband in thin brown leather. The lining is marked to the firm of Georg Teufel (&) Sohn of Tuttlingen. It also bears the marked size '55', and a depot marking 'M 39', denoting Munich, 1939.

(Above) The badge is the second type, with a white eagle on a dark green base, and is hand-sewn to the cap. Note the very rounded shape of the opening edge on the turn-down flap, another early feature – this edge gradually became completely square as the war went on.

Enlisted ranks' tropical field cap *(Tropeneinheitsfeldmütze)*

In 1940, when a German deployment to North Africa was under consideration, a cap was trialled that copied the general form of the *Bergmütze*. The 'universal tropical field cap' was intended to replace the tropical sidecap, and was adopted in 1941 by the Deutsches Afrikakorps. Although resembling the mountain cap, it had a longer peak for protection from the harsh sun. The former's turn-down flap was judged unnecessary, and a doubling of the same shape was simply sewn around the cap as a stiffening panel, with the buttons omitted. The body was made from a hard-wearing olive-brown cotton drill fabric, with a red interior lining. The crown had two zinc ventilation eyelets in each side. The cap proved extremely popular, and cemented the idea for a similarly styled universal field cap, which came to fruition in 1943.

(**Right**) Tropical caps were olive-coloured when issued, but rapidly faded to various shades of tan and beige from the sunlight and from laundering. This process was hastened by the troops' tendency to bleach them deliberately, to give them a 'salty' veteran look. The ubiquitous edelweiss badge is worn on the left side of this cap. Although no Mountain Division was deployed to North Africa, two individual units did serve there between summer 1942 and the Axis surrender in Tunisia in May 1943. Army tropical uniform was also issued to troops serving in Greece and other Mediterranean postings, and to some extent in the far south of the USSR.

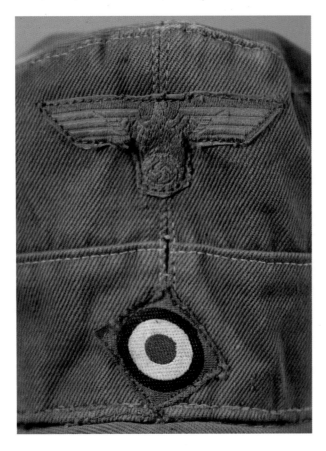

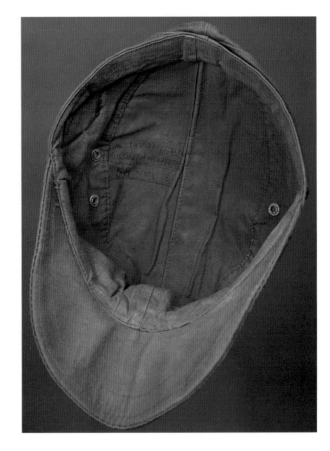

In August 1942 the two German battalions of the unit Sonderverband 288 ('Special Unit 288'), largely raised from German expatriates in Spain and the Middle East, were redesignated as Panzer-Grenadier Regiment (mot) Afrika, within 90. leichte Division. Among the reinforcements shipped to Tunisia in December 1942 was 334. Infanterie Division, which included Gebirgs Infanterie Regiment (mot) 756. This unit distinguished itself in the battle to hold 'Longstop Hill'.

(Bottom far left) The insignia followed the pattern of those made for the field-grey *Feldmütze*, but in the tropical shades of blue-grey on tan-brown. They were BeVo machine-woven, and either machine-sewn with straight or zig-zag stitching, or hand-sewn (especially if removed when bleaching the cap). Early caps featured a soutache of Russia braid sewn in a reversed 'V' of the wearer's Waffenfarbe above the cockade, but this was discontinued in late 1942. Officers wore the same cap but with silver-coloured piping (or gold for generals) around the crown and sometimes round the top edge of the 'scalloped' portion of the dummy flap. However, most officers simply used the enlisted ranks' cap with the piping sewn on by hand.

(Left) The red lining was supposed to provide the best heat protection. Some 1942 versions of the cap had a sweatband of olive-green cloth sewn to a tan leatherette backing strip, but this was soon discontinued. This example bears the maker's stamp of Gustav Thomas of Breslau, with the size '58'. Note the two crimped ventilation eyelets with washers, and the thread sewn through the cap to fix the edelweiss badge.

Snow camouflage headgear

The Gebirgsjäger naturally operated in snow-covered areas where headgear required some level of camouflage. Generally, field-expedient items were improvised, and the main item issued was a white cotton or tricot cover for the *Bergmütze*. This was constructed from two identical pieces of fabric and had an elastic or drawstring around the lower edge. It stretched shapelessly over both the body and peak of the mountain cap, camouflaging its colour and breaking its outline. Interviews with surviving Gebirgsjäger suggest that covers were issued on an 'as required' basis and handed back to unit stores after use. Surviving examples are so rare that the authors have not encountered a single one.

(Right) The cover is seen here worn by a unit about to go on patrol. Note also the snowshoes worn by several of the men; they all wear the three-pocket anorak and matching trousers (see pages 94–97).

(Left) An interesting example of a field-made white camouflage *Bergmütze*. It is constructed of hard-wearing white cotton drill, and imitates the cut of the standard mountain cap, complete with a turn-down flap fastened in this case with a single large white button. The standard edelweiss badge sewn securely to the left side suggests that this cap was actually the property of an individual soldier rather than simply drawn from Kompanie stores.

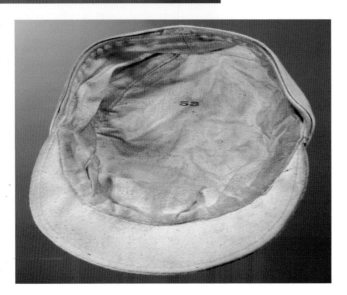

(Right) The interior of the cap shows that it is machine sewn in a semi-professional manner, has no sweatband, and is simply stamped with a head size only.

(Right) An interesting white version of the *Bergmütze* is worn by a Hauptmann of Gebirgsjäger in this newspaper photo taken during the siege of the Cholm Pocket in northern Russia in January–May 1942. Apparently a completely white *Bergmütze* with a two-button flap closure, it is evident in several photos being worn by different ranks. Note that the right-hand officer wearing the *feldgrau* mountain cap displays on his left sleeve the Narvik Shield commemorative award; a similar shield would be instituted in June 1942 for the defenders of Cholm.

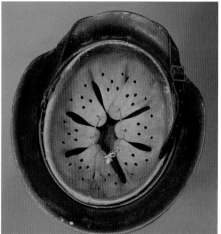

Interior of the 1942-type *Stahlhelm*. The ventilated leather liner was anchored between two concentric rings of zinc-galvanized steel.

(Above) A white-painted example of the July 1942 pattern steel helmet, identifiable from the M35 and M40 by its simplified hot-stamped skull with an out-flaring rim. The Gebirgstruppe were, of course, issued with the *Stahlhelm* like all other branches of the Army. (The issue camouflage anorak had a hood cut to a generous size so as to fit over the helmet if required.) In snow conditions the helmet was routinely painted white for camouflage using water-soluble primer, and the practice was officially ordered in Russia on 18 November 1941. This whitewash was readily available, but in its absence soldiers sometimes used local limewash. Both types of finish were fairly easily scrubbed off when spring returned.

(Right) A soldier on ski patrol wearing a whitewashed helmet. During 1942 a fabric camouflage cover for the helmet (*Stahlhelmüberzüge*) was first issued. Initially made of herringbone twill and later from a stronger cotton duck material, this was printed on one side with a 'splinter' camouflage pattern scaled down from that used on the *Zeltbahn* shelter-quarter. The other, inner side was left plain off-white; and since the cover fitted by means of a simple drawstring under the helmet rim, it was often seen in improvised use white-side-out for winter conditions. (This inner side lacked the foliage attachment loops sewn on the splinter-patterned side, but this was hardly a drawback for snow camouflage.)

SERVICE UNIFORMS

Enlisted ranks' tunic (Feldbluse), Model 1933/35

The new national emblem of Nazi Germany, incorporating an eagle and the swastika symbol of the Nazi Party (NSDAP), was ordered for military caps in February 1934; but it was not until March 1935 that it appeared in cloth form on the tunic, and 30 October that year – seven months after the unveiling of the new Wehrmacht – before its application to all military clothing was ordered. This service tunic (Feldbluse), of the pattern introduced in mid 1933, displays the new emblem on the right breast. The 1933 tunic differed only in details from the previous Reichswehr pattern; of field-green wool, it was of traditional single-breasted cut, with a stand-and-fall collar and four box-pleated patch pockets on the breasts and skirts. The collar was closed by a hook-and-eye at the throat, the front by five metal buttons with a face of pebbled texture, painted matt field-grey. At the end of each cuff there was a 14cm slash opening called an *Ärmelschlitz*, with two internal buttons allowing the cuff to be closed tightly. In 1933 the collar was the same colour as the rest of the tunic, but in 1935 it was (briefly) faced with field-grey badge cloth of a darker shade; this was changed to dark green badge cloth late that year. Although the finer details of the tunic were thus a 'work in progress', it established the style for the wartime German Army, and each German soldier received four tunics when issued with his kit.

(Opposite above) The insignia group. The collar patches are traditional light grey woven *Litzen* (the former 'Guard lace' of royal household regiments, extended to the whole Reichswehr by the new German Republic in May 1919), with a strip or 'highlight' of very light green Waffenfarbe down each bar; they are sewn to lozenge-shaped backings covered in dark green badge cloth. The *Brustadler* national emblem is of the first pattern, in off-white cotton on a light grey base, and is hand sewn to the tunic.

(Opposite) The partial lining of brown drill fabric, reinforcing the shoulders and various seams. Note the pocket closed by a horn button, low inside the front; this contained two field dressings (one each for entry and exit wounds). The end of a pair of rear waist adjustment tapes is just visible protruding from its tunnel at the hip; this was discontinued in early 1936. At the front and rear hips four metal wire hooks are anchored in one of three alternative holes in a strong tape, and pass through stitch-reinforced holes to the outside of the tunic itself (*see* photo, left). These hooks helped distribute the weight of the belt-order to the shoulders.

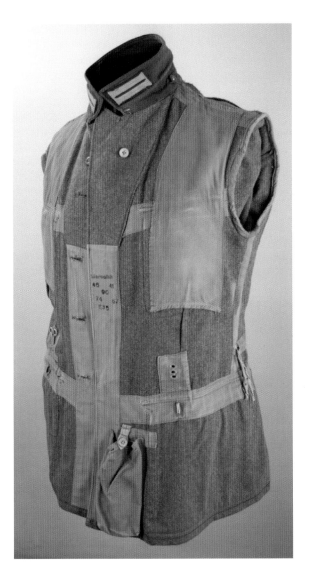

(Below) During 1933–34 the first-pattern shoulder straps changed in quick succession from base cloth (here), to field-grey, and finally to dark green badge cloth; all had a pointed end, no piping, and were secured by a button bearing the company number – here '2' – and a reinforced lower tongue that passed under a 'bridle' tab at the shoulder seam. This example has an early chain-stitched '100' for Gebirgsjäger Rgt 100, in *hell-grün*-coloured thread. This stitching was done after the strap was made, since it shows at the rear.

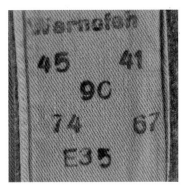

(Left) Markings on the inner right lining panel: the Bavarian maker's name Wernofeh, five size measurements, and the depot stamp 'E35' for Erfurt, 1935.

Officer's parade tunic *(Waffenrock)*

The full dress tunic or *Waffenrock* (literally 'arm of service tunic') was introduced for wear by the Army in June 1935. Its design deliberately evoked memories of the old Imperial German Army, since the new regime understood the value of appealing to patriotic traditions. The tunic was cut from a fine quality field-grey gabardine cloth, and lacked external pockets (there was usually a hidden pocket inside the left breast). It featured dark green badge-cloth facings on the turn-back cuffs and stand-and-fall collar, and piping in the appropriate Waffenfarbe around the top edge of the cuffs, the front and bottom edges of the collar, down the front opening, and around the pair of scalloped vertical rear skirt flaps. The front closed with eight bright silver pebbled-finish buttons.

Parade tunics were cut to fit snugly without creases, for the smartest appearance possible. This example displays a fine hand-embroidered edelweiss sleeve badge on the upper right arm, but this was only introduced in May 1939 and was affixed after that date. Also shown here are the brocade full dress belt and plaited silver cord full dress aiguillettes, introduced for officers in June 1935; these were worn for parades and other formal occasions, as were any awards. The *Waffenrock* was worn with the helmet or service cap, full medals, silver belt and aiguillettes, breeches and riding boots, grey gloves and sword with its knot for the order of dress termed Paradeanzug. Class One ceremonial dress (Grosser Gesellschaftsanzug), for which the helmet was never worn, was otherwise the same above the waist, but with piped straight trousers, shoes and white gloves. Class Two ceremonials (Kleiner Gesellschaftsanzug) differed only in that the ribbons of any medals were worn as a bar in place of the full decorations – here, the Service Medal (awarded for a minimum of four years' service) and the Annexation of Austria Medal. Officer's walking-out dress (Ausgehanzug) was the same as Class Two ceremonials.

(Left) The insignia are hand-embroidered from bright aluminium bullion. The collar patch *Litzen* are worked on a base of Waffenfarbe badge-cloth; note the difference in shades between the *hellgrün* of the collar patch base and the tunic piping; such variations were common, due to the different dyes used by a number of makers. This example of the officer's hand-embroidered bullion eagle shows a slight variation from the standard, with the top of the dark green badge-cloth base trimmed into a raised portion around the eagle's head.

(Below) The shoulder straps for the dress tunic, of bright aluminium wire, were always sewn into the seam at the butt end. Those shown here are for a Reserve-Offizier of Gebirgsjäger Regiment 100; under the usual base of *hellgrün* Waffenfarbe, note the extra layer in light grey, denoting Reserve status.

(Below) The rear skirt had two ornamental flaps that mimicked three-button pockets, with a scalloped edge piped in Waffenfarbe. The upper pair of buttons here were solid, with a 'ramp' behind the top to support the edge of the brocade belt. As the tunic had no external pockets there were usually two hidden pockets inside the skirt on each side of the rear vent. Note also the cuff, ornamented with two rectangular patches of Waffenfarbe *(Ärmelpatten)* showing single straight *Litzen* bars with a button at the top.

Enlisted ranks' *Waffenrock*

The parade tunic for enlisted and NCO ranks was basically of the same design as that for officers, the main differences being the quality of materials and the insignia. The quality of the enlisted ranks' wool tunic was consistently high, nevertheless; regular soldiers were issued with two dress tunics at the depot, and those with the means – including many NCOs – could have their own 'best' tunic privately tailored from officer-quality tricot cloth. The tunic was worn for parades, formal functions, special guard duty and 'walking out'. Not all soldiers were impressed with this tunic, however, since many found it too 'old fashioned' and gaudy; they gave it the derogatory nickname *'Sarrasani'*, inferring that it looked like the ringmaster's costume in a famous German circus.

The tunic shown here is a privately tailored example made in Lauingen, Bavaria, for a Feldwebel of Gebirgsjäger Regiment 98. It conforms to the regulations governing the issue tunic, but shows a higher quality of materials and craftsmanship. The cloth is a fine field-grey gabardine; the tunic is sharply tailored at the waist, and has an internal waistbelt with a metal buckle to ensure a trim fit. The rear skirt has the same scalloped dummy pocket flaps as the officer's pattern, complete with upper ramp buttons to support the service belt. The insignia were similar to those on the officer's tunic, but machine-woven instead of hand-embroidered – although the breast eagle on this piece is in fact a fine officer-quality pattern in bullion embroidery. The actual enlisted ranks' pattern was flat machine-woven in silver wire on a dark green base, which was in turn machine-sewn to an outline patch of dark green badge-cloth. (Some examples show light grey base cloth instead.) The most distinctive mark of NCO status is the use of flat silver *Tresse* or braid on the cuff top and rear and collar top and leading edges, of a special wide 15mm pattern. (That on the shoulder straps retained the standard 9mm measure, however.) This example shows the ribbon for the Iron Cross 2nd Class in the second buttonhole and the Wound Badge in Black on the left breast, below a small ribbon bar for the Service and Austrian Annexation medals.

(Below) The collar and cuff *Litzen* of the enlisted ranks' parade tunic were flat machine-woven on long strips of Waffenfarbe cloth. They were cut from these, then folded and sewn around the backing patch. Just visible here is the characteristic difference between the Waffenfarbe shade of the collar and cuff patches and that of the tunic piping. Note the wider 15mm *Tresse* braid used on the collar and cuffs, compared with the regular 9mm NCO braid on the shoulder straps. The wider braid has two internal rows of diamond patterning as opposed to the single row in the regular braid.

(Above) The shoulder strap for Feldwebel's rank is fully edged with 9mm *Tresse*, and bears one white-metal pip. The numerals denoting Gebirgsjäger Regiment 98 are attached with two flat prongs on the back of each. Numerals and letters were embroidered in Waffenfarbe-coloured thread for ranks from Jäger (private) up to Unteroffizier, and of stamped aluminium for senior NCO ranks from Feldwebel upwards. These early dress straps usually have a fairly rigid internal stiffener, of pasteboard or occasionally wire. Note the outer piping in Waffenfarbe, here made of artificial silk cord rather than the usual wool seen on *Feldblusen*. On parade tunics shoulder straps were always sewn into the shoulder seam at the butt, and secured with an aluminium pebbled-finish button.

(Right) The tunic was made in 1937 by the firm of Feller-Eckert in Lauingen a/D ('on the Donau'). Like most tailored tunics, it has a BeVo machine-woven label at the nape of the neck **(above)** and an owner's nametag in the interior left breast pocket **(below)**. Such tunics also had features such as internal waistbelts for a flattering fit, and a suspension strap with clip for the sword inside the left hip.

Austrian officer's tunic

In the so-called Anschluss of March 1938, Austria was annexed by Germany with the support of a sizeable part of the population, and became part of the German Reich. The Austrian armed forces were incorporated into the Wehrmacht, and would thereafter adopt the uniforms, equipment and standards of the German armed forces. The Austrians had a fine tradition as mountain soldiers, and so it was a foregone conclusion that many Austrian personnel would serve in such formations of the German Army. The Heer immediately received an additional two Gebirgsjäger Divisionen, and others were eventually headquartered on Austrian soil. During an early transition period many Austrian officers wore their former uniform but with German insignia replacing Austrian. The first step was usually simply to add cap and breast eagles to the uniform, but in time many officers – wanting to retain a perfectly good uniform that was already the right colour – had it adapted to conform in general appearance to the German model, and added a full set of German insignia. It was not unusual to see such tunics being worn well into the war years, as a matter of national pride.

The original Austrian tunic had a high collar in the same cloth as the body, so this has been replaced with a fall collar with pointed ends, faced with dark green badge cloth, and adorned with the standard officer's *Litzen* patches with *hellgrün* 'lights'. The tunic pattern shown here originally had a fly front hiding the buttons; this has been modified by sewing in buttonholes for six of the usual pebbled-finish buttons. One of the immediate ways of identifying a former Austrian (or indeed an 'Austrian style') tunic is by the dramatically scalloped pocket flaps, here covering slash pockets in the breasts and skirts. Shoulder straps for Leutnant's rank have been sewn in at the shoulders, and an officer's bullion breast eagle has been added to the breast. The tunic also features an officer's quality edelweiss sleeve badge in silver and gold wire.

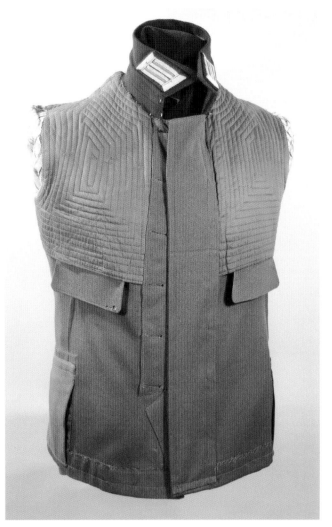

(Above) Note the officer's breast eagle hand-embroidered in bullion wire, simply hand-sewn to the tunic. The very long points of the scalloped pocket flaps were distinctive of both Austrian and Hungarian uniforms.

(Below) Two Austrian enlisted men photographed immediately after the Anschluss have hastily added German national eagle-and-swastika badges to their caps and tunics. Note their own Austrian edelweiss badges on the collar patches – this was the traditional distinction of the old KuK Tyroler Kaiserjäger – and the long-pointed pocket flaps of the Gefreiter on the right, who sports a traditional Austrian army marksmanship lanyard.

(Above) The interior shows very little lining, but many Austrian tunics have this quilted padding at shoulder and breast. Even some German-supplied tunics had this feature retro-fitted, for comfort. Note the two-hook closure of the collar, which has been added to this tunic to replace the former standing type.

(Below) This uniform was found with its owner's former Austrian peaked cap, hastily adapted by the addition of a metal eagle badge from a *Schirmmütze*.

Officer's service tunic *(Feldbluse)*, Model 1936

Several modifications were made to the *Feldbluse* Model 1935 as the need for changes became apparent. The collar had been modified to dark green in 1935; the waist adjustment tapes were eliminated in early 1936, and more extensive lining was ordered later that year. Together these produced the most common pre-war tunic, normally referred to as the M36. While officers were required to procure their own uniforms from either the official outlets or authorized tailors, they were also permitted to purchase enlisted-grade uniforms from their unit's clothing depot and have these modified to reflect their officer status. Officers usually took advantage of this in order to acquire a less expensive tunic for actual wear in the field, and the practice became almost a matter of course during the wartime years.

The tunic shown here is an example of a basic enlisted ranks' tunic that has been carefully modified by a tailor to reflect officer status. The collar has been replaced by a slightly larger one with a more pronounced pointed shape, closing with two hooks-and-eyes. The cuffs have had the *Ärmelschlitz* removed from the rear edge, although – unlike most such adapted tunics – they have not had a matching deep turned-up cuff added to mimic the officer's service tunic. All utility lining and tabs have been removed, and replaced with a grey cotton half-lining that extends from the chest up. The body of the tunic has been extensively re-tailored to improve the cut.

(Left) The insignia follow the regulation form for officers. The collar patches are of silver wire embroidered on a dark green badgecloth base, and bear strips of light green Gebirgsjäger Waffenfarbe down the bars. The standard silver bullion officer's breast eagle is sewn to the right breast; note that the top edge is angled parallel to the ground rather than to the top pocket seam.

(Centre left) The shoulder straps are sewn into the shoulder seam and buttoned close to the collar. Note, again, the contrasting shades of *hellgrün* on these and the 'lights' of the collar *Litzen*. The single gilt-washed pips identify the rank of first lieutenant – Oberleutnant – and a set of stamped gilt-washed numerals show that this officer serves with Gebirgsjäger Regiment 100. This unit was originally part of 1. Gebirgs Division, but was transferred in 1940 to form the nucleus for the infantry brigade of the new 5. Gebirgs Division.

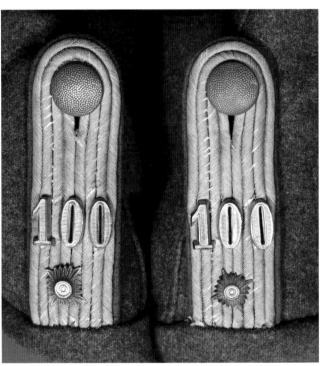

(Left) This officer has purchased a fine hand-woven example of the edelweiss sleeve badge in silver- and gold-coloured bullion.

(Above) The interior of the tunic shows the quite extensive modifications carried out compared with the 'straight from stores' example shown on page 33. The original lining has been replaced with a grey cotton half-lining covering the upper chest and shoulders. The holes for the belt hooks to pass through have been carefully patched from behind. It is apparent that various spare pieces of field-grey fabric have been used in the alterations.

Enlisted ranks' *Feldbluse*, Model 1936

The Model 1936 was the most recognizable tunic the Germans produced, and is easily identified in period photos of the annexation of Austria or Czechoslovakia, the war in Poland or the invasion of France and the Low Countries. It was smart, practical and comfortable. The tunic was cut in *feldgrau* wool and had four box-pleated patch pockets. The front closed with five pebbled-finish buttons painted field-grey (although examples of manufacturers' variations with six buttons are known). The fall-down collar was of dark green cloth, as were the shoulder straps. The interior

of the Model 1933 tunic was upgraded in December 1936 to provide additional protection from wear, including lining panels to both front sides as well as the back. This lining was made of a strong cotton drill in shades varying from brown to a beige-grey colour. At breast height front and back there were openings to allow the belt hook suspension tapes *(Tragegurte)* to pass through the lining and up over the shoulders. Along the length of these tapes 15 reinforced eyelets allowed adjustable suspension of the wire belt hooks *(Seitenhaken)*.

(Left) The new 1938 universal pattern enlisted ranks' collar patches *(Einheitslitzen)* replaced the two strips of the appropriate Waffenfarbe down the bars with dark green for all arms of service. The round-ended November 1938 shoulder straps had a base of dark green badgecloth, and – since the arm of service was no longer identifiable from the collar patches – piping in the wearer's Waffenfarbe all round the outside edges except for the butt end. The internal stiffener was discontinued; note the attachment tongue with its brown cotton backing, and an early button with the numeral '1' for 1. Kompanie. In 1935 the first-pattern light grey breast eagle was replaced with a flat machine-woven badge in off-white on a dark green base. Machine-woven variations also exist in white cotton on dark-green wool, and these appear to have been popular with NCO ranks.

(Left) This edelweiss badge, machine-woven on dark green backing, was the most common type for enlisted ranks early in the war. It is worn centred on the upper right sleeve.

(Below) The inner right lining is stamped with the size numbers and the depot stamp 'St. 40', for Stettin, 1940. Note the medical dressing pocket marked with the manufacturer's name 'Franz Krämer'.

(Above) The new and more extensive lining. Note the belt hook suspension tapes emerging from slits in the lining after passing over the shoulders, to spread the weight of the belt equipment worn in the field. The many eyelets allowed adjustable positioning of the hooks according to the wearer's build; each hook then passed through one of the reinforced holes that were set in four vertical lines of three, each side of the front and back of the waist. Note also the detachable white collar liner, which was buttoned to the inside of the tunic collar to protect it from sweat stains and to protect the soldier's neck from chafing – the issue shirt was collarless at this date.

Officer's piped service tunic *(geschmückte Feldbluse)*

In July 1937 this optional 'ornamented field tunic' was introduced to bridge the gap between the *Waffenrock* and the *Feldbluse*. It differed from the latter only in having piping in the wearer's Waffenfarbe added around the bottom and leading edges of the collar, the top of the turn-back cuffs and down the left edge of the front opening. Since it was an option for formal dress those officers who chose to acquire one paid for it from their uniform allowance or out of their own pocket.

The 'ornamented' tunic could be worn with trousers and shoes for both classes of Gesellschafts-anzug ceremonial dress and for walking-out dress, but not for Paradeanzug. There was also a 'reporting order' of dress (Meldeanzug) for officers: this comprised the peaked service cap, either the parade *Waffenrock* or this piped tunic, belt, breeches and riding boots, grey gloves, sword and knot. Full medals were never to be worn on the breast of this tunic, only their ribbons, although pin-back decorations could be displayed.

(**Left**) The dress tunic is generally found with quite a stiff collar, with slightly more pointed ends than on the regular service tunic. The collar patches are hand-embroidered in silver bullion wire on dark green badge-cloth over a cardboard template. The base cloth was then cut and glued over a buckram backing which stiffens the insignia. Here the Waffenfarbe strips along the *Litzen* bars are of dress-quality silk; on the service tunic they are often simple twist cord or 'Russia braid'.

(**Left**) This breast eagle is a fine example of high quality hand embroidery. The differing patterns of wire are sewn through the dark green cloth base over a shaped cardboard template in order to maintain consistency and size. Many examples are sealed at the back with an embroiderer's paper tape, to prevent thread pulls.

(**Right**) This is a particularly noteworthy example of the variation of Waffenfarbe colours found on Gebirgsjäger uniforms: three distinct shades of green can be seen on the shoulder straps, collar piping and *Litzen* on a garment that remains unaltered since the war. The official colour for all Jäger (light infantry) and Gebirgsjäger (mountain light infantry) was 'light green' *(hellgrün)*. However, a similar branch colour existed from mid 1939 when Rifle regiments (Schützen-Regimenter) were awarded Waffenfarbe in so-called 'meadow-green' *(weisengrün)*. In mid 1942 this was extended to motorized infantry, when the Rifle units were redesignated as Panzer-grenadiere. The new 'meadow-green' was a more apple-green shade, lighter than the 'light green' of the Gebirgsjäger, which was in fact a medium green. Due to the complications of supply and variations in dye batches the shades of *hellgrün* actually found on uniforms are anything but consistent. In this photo the Waffenfarbe strips on the collar bars are for all intents in the *weisengrün* of the Panzergrenadiers. The shoulder strap base is a good example of what is generally accepted as *hellgrün*; and the collar piping is in a shade between the other two applications.

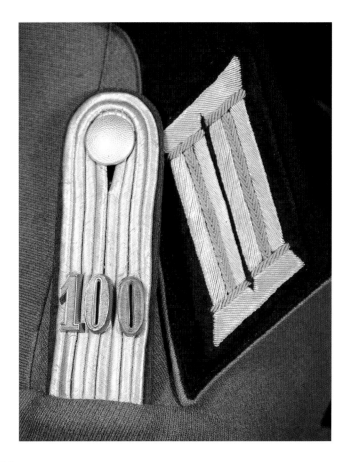

Tropical service tunic

In 1940, when the German Army had to envisage the possibility of going to the assistance of their Italian allies in North Africa, consideration began of a suitable design for a tropical service uniform *(Tropenanzug)* for combat in hotter climates. Research and development was carried out at the Hamburg Tropical Institute, and in February 1941 the first German soldiers to disembark at Tripoli in Libya were wearing the new uniform. Although only a few mountain units served in Africa, this uniform went on to be worn around the Mediterranean theatre and in the hotter southern zones of the Eastern Front.

The tunic was cut much like the service tunic, with four pleated patch pockets (first pattern), but it had a permanently open collar. The fabric used was a hard-wearing cotton drill in drab olive, but with wear this often faded paler. The cuffs had the usual *Ärmelschlitz* vents with pressed paper buttons, and the pocket flaps of the first model were scalloped as on the service tunic. The interior, however, was markedly different. In place of the standard lining there were sand-coloured drill reinforcing panels under each arm, and at the front edge of each pocket flap seam. A buttoning medical dressing pocket was found in the usual place, at the lower right front corner. The tunic had only two belt hook suspenders, one at each hip, hanging from a single permanent tape that extended from the armpit seam down to the usual three reinforced holes at the waist, where the hooks protruded to support the belt kit. Subdued tropical insignia were developed; these were flat machine-embroidered and followed the basic design of those for the continental uniform, but in different colours. The collar *Litzen* were a light blue-grey colour with sand-colour strips and centre, sewn directly to the collar without backing. The breast eagle was blue-grey on a mustard-coloured base.

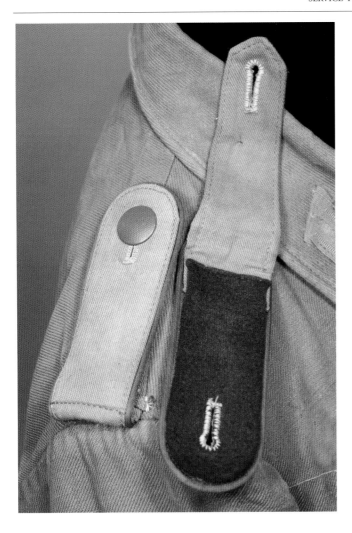

(Left) Shoulder straps were of the same design as those for continental uniform, but were made from offcuts of the olive-drab cloth during tunic construction. They had the usual Waffenfarbe piping and were detachable in the usual way. Note the olive-brown tropical greatcoat wool used for the underlay.

(Below) The very basic lining, showing the reinforcing patches under the arms and behind the leading pocket seams. Note the medical dressing pocket, and the belt suspension hooks hanging below the armpit. The cloth strip at the shoulders covers the 'S'-clip that retains the shoulder strap button, to prevent it rubbing.

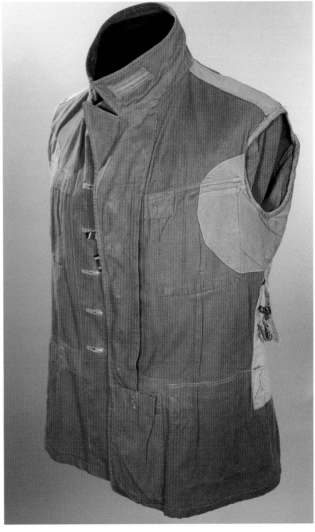

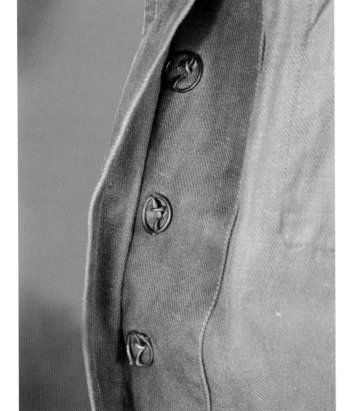

(Left) All buttons were painted sand-brown and were removable; the shanks passed through eyelet holes, and were retained inside by 'S'-shaped wire clips. The clips for the five front buttons were hidden behind this interior fly flap.

(Above) Details of the typical wartime machine-embroidered edelweiss patch, and of the 'Afrikakorps' cuff title. This was introduced for eligible soldiers in July 1941, but was replaced in January 1943 by the 'Afrika' title, which was a service award rather than simply an identification.

Officer's lightweight field service tunic

Early in the war (and occasionally even before it broke out), it became fashionable for officers and senior NCOs to privately provide themselves with a lightweight service tunic for wear in the warmer months. These tended to be made from materials like groundsheet cloth, a hard-wearing cotton fabric that was readily available. The colours ranged from early light grey, through olive-green, to the mustard-brown of the Reichs Arbeitsdienst (National Labour Service, RAD) and captured Soviet groundsheets. It is often possible to find stitching holes in the cloth from its previous use. Thes lightweight garments are usually cut exactly like the *Feldbluse;* a collar of dark green badgecloth, often fashionably pointed, was usually added. The use of these tunics appears to have been tolerated, especially for wear in the field, since they were popular with all ranks from senior NCO to general.

This example is made from a sturdy olive-green cotton drill and follows the accepted form of the service tunic. The four patch pockets have box pleats and scalloped flaps, and the cuffs have deep turn-ups. A dark green pointed collar is stiffened with a rigid interlining material to preserve the shape, and closed with two hooks-and-eyes (many such tunics have only one). As a rule these tunics are found with little or no interior lining, but this example is lined from the chest up with *feldgrau* wool stitched with a quilted pattern. This appears to be more of an effort to preserve the shape of the tunic than a protection against cool weather. Some tunics have simple drill panels to protect the underarms, or pads at the shoulders to make them sit well. Others even have a slit for a sword- or dagger-hanger, showing that they were popular even for walking-out dress. The quality of such tunics varies depending on the skill of the tailor and the budget of the wearer, from very fine to almost 'field made'.

(**Opposite**) Awards were worn on these tunics as on those of normal weight. While some wool tunics had the pins for awards pushed through the fabric, generally extra cotton loops were sewn on for mounting, as shown here. Often the size and spacing of such loops can give an indication of the awards bestowed on the wearer. Note the quality of the tailoring details displayed on this piece.

(Left) Supporting and service units within the structure of a Gebirgs Division were identified by their own branch's Waffenfarbe – red for Gebirgs Artillerie, black for Gebirgs Pioniere, lemon-yellow for Gebirgs Nachrichten, and so forth. The typical layout of insignia shown here denotes an Oberleutnant in Gebirgs Artillerie Rgt 112, the integral artillery unit of 3. Gebirgs Division. The silver bullion collar *Litzen* have bright red (*hochrot*) Waffenfarbe highlights. The shoulder straps, with the same colour underlay, are sewn directly into the seams; the cords are in subdued silver finish for field wear. A single aluminium pip identifies the rank, below dull gilt-washed regimental numerals. An average quality hand-embroidered eagle is sewn to the right breast.

(Below) The lining panel in field-grey wool covers the complete interior from the chest up. The stitching pattern secures an interlining material, indicating that the lining is more for maintaining the integrity of the tunic's shape than for warmth.

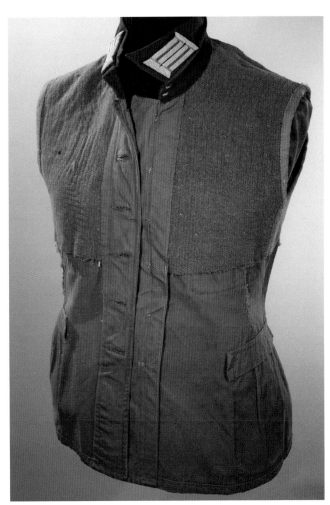

(Centre left) The edelweiss sleeve badge is a machine-woven example typical of those worn by all ranks. Many officers also purchased privately made hand-embroidered examples in metallic threads, even for these lightweight uniforms.

Enlisted ranks' hot weather field service tunic

The increasing use of the old herringbone twill drill uniform as an expedient hot weather combat tunic made it apparent that the troops required something better to replace the woollen *Feldbluse* for summer field use. In early 1942 a lightweight herringbone twill combat uniform was introduced, cut identically to the woollen tunic but with a minimal interior, and this proved very popular. Initially it had four box-pleated patch pockets but – like the tropical tunic – later production examples lost first the pleats and then the scalloped shape of the flaps. The collar could be worn fastened to the throat with a hook-and-eye, but was more usually worn open.

While the addition of insignia to the original drill tunics had been against regulations, the 1942 purpose-made garment was intended to be fully badged, and bridle loops for attached shoulder straps were factory-fitted. The collar insignia were the standard Einheitslitzen, which from the end of 1940 were applied directly to the collar without backing patches; the dark green highlights on the bars had also been replaced with simple dark grey. The breast eagle was applied directly above the right breast pocket.

(Left) The insignia are for a Feldwebel and officer candidate *(Offiziersbewerber)* of Gebirgs Pioniere, as indicated by the black Waffenfarbe piping on the standard shoulder straps, outside the usual 9mm *Tresse* NCO braid. Officer candidates were identified by a double loop of *Tresse* sewn around the base of the straps; sometimes this was a single braid loop with a black dividing line down the centre, sometimes – as here – two separate strips. The collar has standard *Tresse* edging; note the plain dark grey lights on the basic factory-applied *Einheitslitzen*. The light grey Bevo-woven breast eagle has by this date lost its dark green base, replaced with a standard drab green colour.

(Below left) The traditional badge is another of several wartime variations, machine-embroidered on field-grey wool backing, which gives it a more subdued look. Most badges are hand-sewn to the sleeve, but this example has been expertly machine-sewn with zig-zag stitching.

(Below) The minimal lining closely resembles that of the tropical tunic *(see* page 37), with reinforced armpits and leading pocket seams. This lining was made either from cotton drill like that of the tropical tunic, or from the silver-grey cellulose artificial satin fabric seen in many other wartime tunics. Again like the tropical tunic, for ease of cleaning the buttons were all removable, the shanks being secured behind a front fly flap with 'S'-shaped wire split pins; some tunics had five, others six buttons. The two belt hook suspenders were also arranged and attached like those on the tropical tunic, hanging above each hip. Note also the buttons provided for attaching a collar liner.

Enlisted ranks' *Feldbluse*, Model 1943

The standard issue *Feldbluse* underwent a number of changes during the war years, as the Reich attempted to save resources and as factories employed less skilled labour. In 1940 the dark green badgecloth on the collar was eliminated, and replaced with the same *feldgrau* cloth as used for the rest of the tunic. During 1941 the number of front buttons was increased to six, a measure thought to be a reflection of the declining cloth quality. In late 1942–early 1943 the pleats on all four pockets were discontinued; initially the flaps remained scalloped, as in this example, but by late 1943 they were simply straight-cut.

The quality of fabrics used in uniform production declined steadily during the war years, as demands on all kinds of raw material supplies sky-rocketed. The basic cloth was increasingly made from reconstituted wool, with old woollen fabrics being pulped and rolled into bolts of field-grey cloth. The resulting material had poorer insulation qualities and was less resilient, especially when wet. Close examination of mid- to late-wartime garments made from this fabric shows small flecks of undyed scrap in the weave. After some months of wear in the field the appearance of such uniforms was usually much degraded.

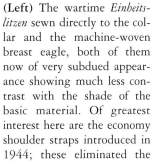

(Left) The wartime *Einheitslitzen* sewn directly to the collar and the machine-woven breast eagle, both of them now of very subdued appearance showing much less contrast with the shade of the basic material. Of greatest interest here are the economy shoulder straps introduced in 1944; these eliminated the underlay, leaving the raw edge of the piping exposed each side of a centred strip of artificial satin running the full length of strap and tongue. The authors have seen bundles of tunics taken from a factory at the end of the war with these straps already in place, ready for delivery to stores.

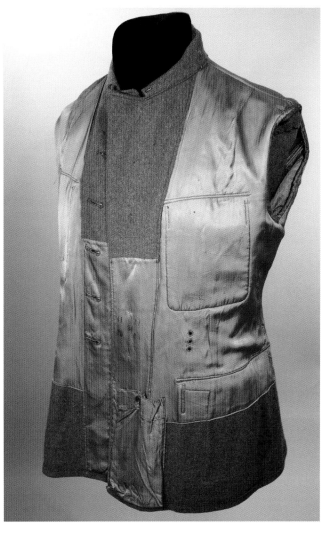

(Right) The interior also underwent changes. The long over-the-shoulder tapes for the belt support hooks were discontinued for most troops as early as mid 1939, and replaced with permanently fixed straps (missing from this example). These were often made from the old recycled support straps, and simply sewn to the body of the tunic above the three belt hook holes. The earlier cotton drill used for tunic linings gave way to an artificial satin material made from cellulose fibre, the forerunner of rayon. (Commercial items such as toothbrushes and stockings were being made of an artificial thread called Purlon.) The artificial satin fabric seen here in the lining may be found in various colours, from this light gunmetal shade to silver-grey or a deep bronze.

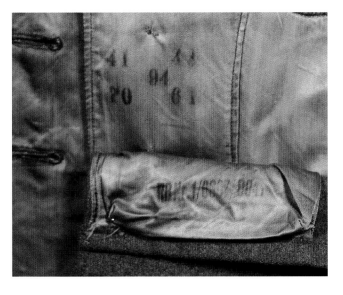

(Left) The usual set of size measurements are shown on the edge of the front right panel. Note below these, on the base of the medical dressing pocket, a *Reichsbetriebsnummer*, abbreviated to *RbNr* followed by a long series of digits. This system of manufacturer numbering was introduced early in 1943 for security reasons, replacing the manufacturers' name and location stamps.

Officer's *Feldbluse*, Model 1944

In 1943 selected troops on the Eastern front trialed a new service tunic which marked a striking change in the German soldier's style of uniform. This garment represented an attempt at standardization across all branches of the Wehrmacht, and the introduction of a design that was more economical and easier to make than the old four-pocket, long-skirted type. The new design was accepted and put into production in 1944, and became universally known as the M44 uniform. However, its use never became widespread enough to markedly change the appearance of the German services, as existing stocks of the old four-pocket tunic had to be used up first. (Translation from German nomenclature can be confusing. In English usage a 'tunic' implies a crotch-length garment, which in the US Army is called a 'coat'. From 1938 a 'blouse' was the British term for a waist-length garment, like the upper part of the new British Army 'battledress, serge' introduced in that year. The later US Army copy of this was termed a 'field jacket'; but in German *'Bluse'* was used for both waist- and crotch-length styles.)

The new *Feldbluse* followed the Allied trend towards a waist-length 'battledress' style, eliminating the lower skirt completely to produce a short, single-breasted jacket with two patch breast pockets. The collar was cut to be worn open with the lapels folded back, but could be buttoned up to the throat in cold weather. The front was provided with six buttons, the lower two being set on a notably deep waistband. Belt hook suspenders were at only two points, one on each hip. The sleeves retained the adjustable cuff vent but with a much simplified design; the buttonholes pierced the cuff itself, allowing it to be either tightened or worn open. The M44 style seems to have been accepted readily enough by officers (even some generals) and enlisted ranks alike, as having a more modern appearance. This example is for an Oberleutnant of Gebirgsjäger, and is an issue item adapted for an officer's use. The fabric is a hard-wearing tricot material known as *'Italienischer Stoff'*, after the uniform cloth used by the Italian Army. Huge quantities of this material were captured when the Italians surrendered to the Allies and the Germans occupied the country in the autumn of 1943, and once stocks ran low the Germans actually developed and produced an identical fabric of their own. The cloth presents a blue-grey colour, and both a smooth tricot and a coarse, stiff wool may be found. Many Waffen-SS field tunics were produced in this fabric. After September 1944 officers were required to have their tunics made to the M44 cut rather than in the old four-pocket style.

(Left) Insignia were worn in the same configuration as on the M36 tunic. These officer *Litzen* are made with Waffenfarbe highlights of 'Russia braid'. The breast eagle is of average quality, in aluminium bullion. The shoulder straps are also of late war quality, showing a crude, wide felt base. The cord tops are subdued, and display the single pip of Oberleutnant. The pressed white metal numeral '1' is unexplained; these cyphers identified Regimenter or Abteilungen, but not higher formations such as divisions.

(Right) The interior lining of the new pattern *Feldbluse* is made here from a bronze-coloured artificial silk. It basically mimics the upper part of the lining of the old service tunic, covering the shoulders and edging the front opening, and it has belt hook suspenders hanging beneath the armpits. However, due to the lack of the two exterior skirt pockets, two buttoning internal chest pockets are now provided, directly behind the external breast pockets.

(Left) There is little doubt that this fine bullion officer's edelweiss sleeve badge was taken from a previous uniform for use on this late-war garment. It displays the finest hand embroidery executed in both silver and gold metallic threads. Such quality was rarely seen this late in the war.

Enlisted ranks' *Feldbluse*, Model 1944

The new Model 1944 field tunic was intended for wear by all ranks and all branches of the Wehrmacht who wore the field-grey service dress. While it was made in several different fabrics including the so-called *'Italienischer Stoff'*, it was intended to be mass-produced in a wool termed *Feldgrau 44*. This was actually an olive-brown reconstituted woollen material, and it was used in the production of caps, trousers, tunics and enlisted ranks' shoulder straps. However, with large stocks of the older fabric to be used up, it never fully changed the generally field-grey tone of Army uniforms.

The tunic buttoned from the waist, with two buttons on the waistband and four above this; the top one was redundant except when the tunic was closed to the throat. Further to this there was a buttoning tab under the left collar point, with a corresponding button opposite to allow the collar to be turned up and fastened across the chin. Many of the pebbled-finish exterior buttons found on the M44 were of a new economy type, with a wire shank shaped like a 'bale handle'. At the base of each cuff there was a vent with a button sewn to the inner edge, facing two alternative buttonholes in the hem of the cuff, allowing it to be closed loosely or tightly around the wrist. The cuff and internal pocket buttons were usually made of either vulcanized rubber or pressed paper. The interior lining consisted of panels that covered the shoulders from the breast up, a vertical reinforcing panel on either side of the front opening, and two internal patch pockets with simple button closure. Under each armpit hung the suspension tape for the belt hook; there were generally two alternative holes at each hip for the hooks to pass through.

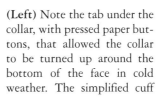

(Left) Note the tab under the collar, with pressed paper buttons, that allowed the collar to be turned up around the bottom of the face in cold weather. The simplified cuff vent – *Ärmelschlitz* – has the button inside the vent with two facing buttonholes for an adjustable fit sewn directly through the cuff.

(Above) Insignia followed the same layout as on earlier service tunics. Note the absence of *Tresse* NCO braid edging to the collar. As often seen, this NCO has continued to wear his early dark green-based shoulder straps, with Waffenfarbe piping and the *Tresse* for the rank of Unteroffizier. Note the new form of breast eagle introduced in 1944, which simplified attachment with a triangular backing rather than one following the outline of the eagle.

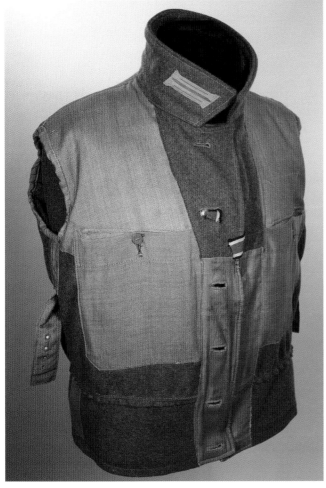

Left) The simplified lining of the short M44 *Feldbluse*. The interior pockets are placed directly in line with the external ones, and close with a pressed paper button. This simple brushed artificial silk lining extends over the shoulders, with reinforcement patches at various points; the two belt hook suspenders extend from the armpit seams. There is an RBNr marking on the front right reinforcement panel; and note the method of attaching the ribbon for the Iron Cross 2nd Class.

The actual shades of the colour that is usually simply termed *feldgrau* varied appreciably over the period 1933-45. Caps, tunics and trousers wore out and were replaced at different times, so from head to ankle a soldier might present three distinctly different shades. Most such variations occurred more or less at random, though general chronological trends during the middle and late war years are apparent. The differences can best be appreciated when uniform items are photographed together in identical light conditions.

(**Above**) The contrasting appearance of two different *Bergmützen*; and of the thin 'reed-green' *(schilfgrün)* drill cloth tunic on the left, with the increasingly shoddy 'field-grey' wool of an M43 tunic on the right. Note the machine-embroidered rank pip of a senior private – Oberjäger – centred on the upper left sleeve. (**Right**) The brownish-olive shade of so-called '*Feldgrau 44*' is more apparent in this Unteroffizer dog-handler's M44 *Feldbluse* when compared with his earlier production field-grey *Berghose*.

INSIGNIA

Edelweiss sleeve badges

The edelweiss sleeve badge was introduced in May 1939 for wear by all ranks currently serving in the Mountain Troops. It took the form of a 6cm × 5cm oval patch displaying an edelweiss flower with white petals, a cluster of yellow stamens in the centre, and a green stem with two leaves. This central motif was surrounded by a white border representing an intertwined pair of climbing ropes. At the base these formed a smaller pair of scissor-shaped loops, and at the top they passed through a climber's piton. The backing matrial was originally dark green badge cloth, but this gradually gave way to field-grey. The badge was worn by all ranks centred on the upper right sleeve of the great-coat, and on all tunics except the drill/fatigue uniform. All ranks wore the same quality of machine-made badge, but hand-embroidered versions in metallic threads could be purchased privately for tailored uniforms; such high quality pieces are usually found on officers' tunics. Other examples are encountered that have regular cotton embroidery except for the piton, which is picked out in silver thread. As seen here, the badges were originally machine-embroidered on wool, but subsequently machine-woven into thinner material.

(Top row) These are examples of the privately embroidered type, showing a number of typical minor variations.

(Central row) Examples of the general issue type worn by all ranks prior to and earlier in the war. This is the type most often encountered.

(Bottom row) These pieces are of more basic type produced in the later war years, on 'field-grey' backing – though actually these will be found in a range of shades showing differing degrees of green, grey and brown in the hue.

Shoulder straps *(Schulterklappen)*

Shoulder straps – sometimes called by collectors 'shoulder boards' in the case of officer ranks in reference to their stiff underlay – were worn by all ranks. Their purpose was originally to indicate the wearer's unit by displaying the numerals of Regimenter and Abteilungen or the cyphers of other military establishments. After the removal of Waffenfarbe highlights from the collar *Litzen* of enlisted ranks in 1938, they also identified the arm of service. The junior enlisted ranks were identified by left sleeve insignia in the form of chevrons and pips, and not by the shoulder straps. All NCO ranks were distinguished by 9mm silver *Tresse* braid around the edges of the shoulder straps, but the most junior rank, Unteroffizier, lacked this across the butt end. Privates' and junior NCOs' straps had Waffenfarbe numerals and cyphers; from Feldwebel upwards these were white metal, and the exact grade was indicated by white metal pips. Junior officer ranks, from Leutnant to Hauptmann, wore straps with a Waffenfarbe underlay completely faced with silver cord in a doubled 'Russia braid' form; exact ranks were indicated by no, one or two yellow-metal pips. Field ranks, from Major to Oberst, wore straps with shorter, stiffened Waffenfarbe underlay, exposed at the butt end, and faced with intertwined silver cord extending beyond the underlay into a buttonhole at the inner end; again, the exact rank was identified by yellow-metal pips. The photographs on this page show a selection of shoulder straps for Mannschaften, and on the opposite page, for Unteroffiziere and Offiziere.

(Right) *Left to right:*
(1 & 2) First pattern, worn 1934–38; Gebirgsjäger Rgt 137. Note pointed end and absence of Waffenfarbe piping.
(3 & 4) Transitional pattern, as seen briefly in 1938–39; Gebirgsjäger Rgt 138. Note rounded end, absence of piping, face in early mid-green badge cloth, underside in 'stone-grey'.
(5 & 6) Second pattern, 1938–40; Gebirgsjäger Rgt 98. Note later dark green face, field-grey underside, and *hellgrün* Waffenfarbe piping.

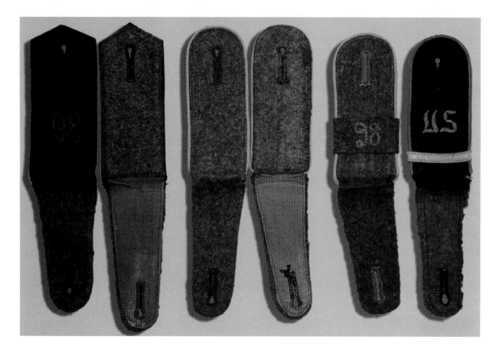

(Left) (1 & 2) First pattern, 1934-38; Gebirgsjäger Rgt 98. (3 & 4) Second pattern, 1940–45, with later *feldgrau* face. Chainstitched regimental numbers were ordered discontinued, for security reasons, in 1940. (5) Second pattern, 1940–45, field-grey, with removable slide for Gebirgsjäger Rgt 98. These temporary designators replaced the chainstitched numerals from 1940, for use when out of the combat zone. (6) Second pattern, with fairly crudely – perhaps locally – chainstitched Gothic cypher 'US' for Unteroffizierschule (NCO School). The single braid round the butt identifies the wearer as an Unteroffizieranwärter (NCO aspirant).

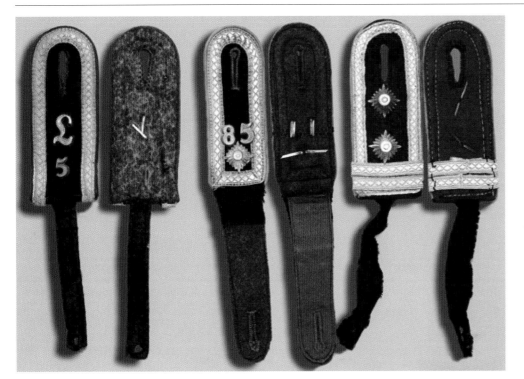

(Left)

(1 & 2) Unteroffizier, 5. Kompanie, Lehr Bataillon – Gebirgsjäger Schule Mittenwald. Originally sewn-in straps, converted for field use with an added tongue.

(3 & 4) Feldwebel, Gebirgs Jäger Rgt 85. Note the odd, very pale shade of the piping.

(5 & 6) Oberfeldwebel – again, converted sewn-in straps with retro-fitted tongues. The double braid round the butt identifies a Fahnenjunker (officer candidate).

(Right)

(1 & 2) Tropical straps, Stabsfeldwebel. Note the mustard-coloured *Tresse* and brown wool underside.

(3 & 4) Unteroffizier of a Gebirgsjägerschule. The shape of the Gothic 'S' (for *Schule*) and the stitching visible underneath show that the cyphers were embroidered some time after the straps were made. Normally the chain-stitch cannot be seen on the reverse side.

(5 & 6) Greenish canvas drill straps for wear on the mountain troops wind jacket, by a Feldwebel of a Gebirgsjägerschule.

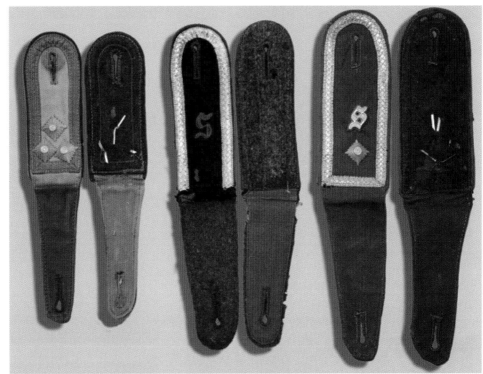

(Left)

(1 & 2) Major, Gebirgsjäger Rgt 100. These early straps are in bright aluminium thread for dress wear; the cloth bar extension at the butt allowed easy removal from the officer's white summer tunic.

(3 & 4) Wartime straps for a Leutnant; note subdued matt-finish cord for field wear. (5 & 6) Very worn example of a Leutnant's matt-finish straps. Note the typical variations in the shades of light green Waffenfarbe seen on the underlays of all the straps illustrated.

TROUSERS

Piped parade/walking-out trousers

All soldiers were issued with a pair of long trousers ornamented with a line of Waffenfarbe piping down the outside seams, for wear on special guard duty and parade, and for walking out. Apart from this piping they were identical to the normal service dress trousers. Before the outbreak of the war the trousers were manufactured in a colour described as *steingrau* or 'stone-grey'. During wartime the manufacturers switched to cloth of the standard grey-green *feldgrau* of the uniform tunics – although men who already had the old pattern might continue to use them, particularly with walking-out dress. The trousers had straight legs, and were cut several centimetres higher at the rear of the waist (*see* the similar effect on the *Berghose* illustrated on page 54).

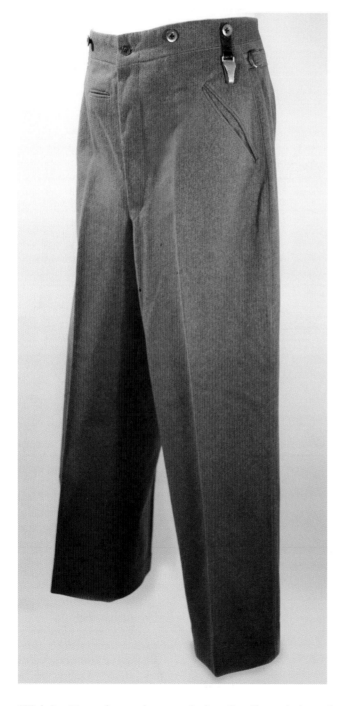

(**Left & below**) The parade trousers buttoned behind a fly front, and had four pairs of buttons spaced around the front and rear waistband for attachment of braces (suspenders). A small buckled size-adjustment tab was provided at each hip. There was a slash pocket at each hip; one horizontal pocket at the right buttock; and a small watch pocket at the right groin – this usually had a small watch-fob loop above it. The example shown here also has a privately acquired button-on suspender and clip for the attachment of a dress sword or dagger through a slit in the tunic. These dress weapons were part of the regulation walking-out uniform.

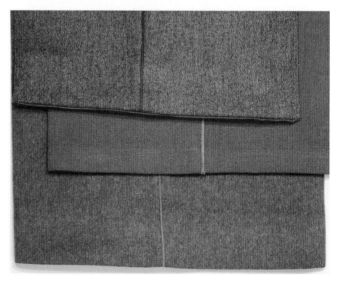

(**Right**) Note here three examples of the parade trousers made with markedly differing shades of uniform cloth, and also of the Waffenfarbe out-seam piping.

Mountain trousers *(Berghose)* for general officer

The 'mountain trousers' issued to the Gebirgstruppe were unique to that arm of service, and – like the *Bergmütze* – were a proud sign of the mountain troops' special status. Like the Luftwaffe's paratroopers, they felt that they cut a more virile and devil-may-care figure with their specially shaped, practically designed trousers gathered at the ankle into low boots, in comparison with the mass of troops wearing general issue trousers stuffed into the high, rather ungainly marching boots. The *Berghose* were of a similar design to the civilian ski trousers of the 1930s. They were cut generously in the leg to allow for unhampered movement, but were tapered in from above the ankle to allow them to be worn tucked into ski- or climbing boots and sealed with low puttees, in order to keep out the snow. The pair shown here were privately tailored for a general officer, using a high quality tricot fabric, and do not conform exactly to the regulation pattern (illustrated on pages 54–56). The waist is cut to a level outline, and has loops for a belt.

(Left & below) These trousers have two slash hip pockets, one horizontal right rear pocket, and a watch pocket at front right. At each hip a small cloth tab engaging with a blued metal patent buckle is provided for size adjustment. The front closes with buttons behind a fly, with a blued metal hook-and-loop at the top. The most striking feature is, of course, the traditional general officers' leg stripes – *Lampassen* – as worn on all uniform trousers and breeches, in bright red *(hochrot)*. Down each leg the outseam is piped in red, and flanked by two broad stripes. The close-up photo below shows the high quality of both the materials and the tailoring of this splendid piece.

(Right) The legs taper sharply at the ankle, and each cuff has an elasticated stirrup that passes under the foot, preventing the leg riding up and pulling out of the top of the ankle-length mountain boots.

Mountain trousers *(Berghose)*

The mountain trousers issued only to the Gebirgsjäger were so well thought of that later in the war they became the model for a new design issued to all troops. Made of stone-grey and later green-grey wool, these *Berghose* were designed specifically for the needs of mountain soldiers, with a high waist to ensure that the top was always covered by the tunic skirt; the wide-cut legs allowed freedom of movement, and were tapered to the ankle, where an outside vent was closed with two tie-tapes. There was a large oval reinforcement panel covering the seat, crotch and inner thighs to protect against hard wear. The pockets all had buttoning flaps, of a slightly scalloped shape, to keep out the elements.

(Left, below & opposite) Note (below) the high-cut profile at the back of the *Berghose,* and the outline of the doubled reinforcement below the seat. Metal washer buttons were provided around the waistband for the attachment of braces (suspenders), and adjustment tapes at each hip – on this example, with blued metal friction buckles; the pocket buttons here are of grey horn. Note the less pronounced scallop of the pocket flaps, the small watch pocket in the right groin with a buttoned flap, and – just visible above its outer end – a small loop for anchoring a fob chain.

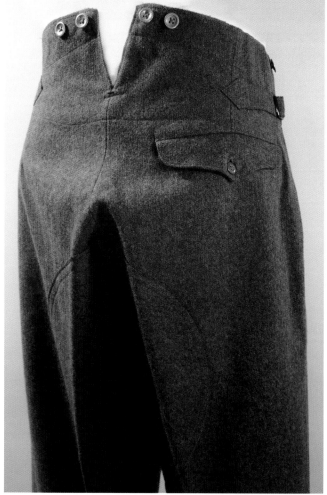

(Right) These trousers show a not uncommon modification to the bottom of the legs. The factory tightening tapes have been removed, and leather strapping with a buckle has been sewn around the base of each leg. Note, at bottom right, the large bright metal clothing hook; these were added so that the trouser cuff could be secured to the boot, preventing it riding up. This pair has lost the stirrups under the foot.

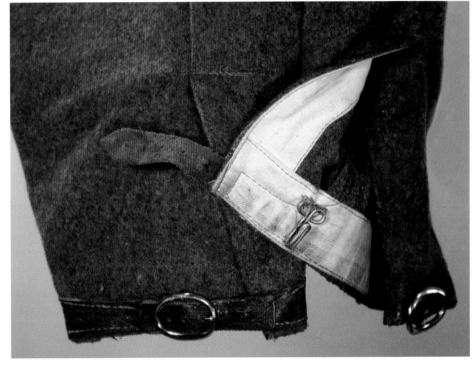

(Left) The right inner waistband shows the size markings, and the stamp of the manufacturer – Tiller AG of Wien (Vienna). However, the depot stamp is 'WB 40', for Würzburg, 1940. Note the off-white cotton drill used for the waistband lining and the pocket bags.

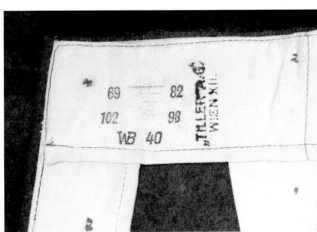

Berghose

(Left & below) This pair of mid-war issue mountain trousers allows comparison with the earlier piece on pages 54–55. The wool is now more field-grey in colour and slightly rougher in texture, but overall the quality is still good. Note that this example retains the cloth stirrups, which pass under the foot and then lace at the outside end through two eyelets next to the cuff vent.

(Above & right) These *Berghose* are depot-stamped 'M42' for Munich, 1942; many of the Gebirgstruppe units had their headquarters depots in Bavaria. This example has pocket bags made of brown cotton drill.

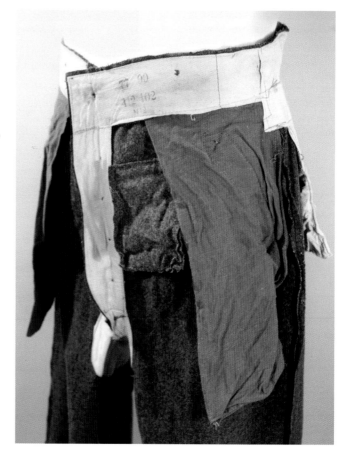

General issue field trousers (*Rundbundhose*), 1943

(Left, below & bottom) During 1943 a new set of trousers were introduced for all troops; modelled on the *Berghose*, these were intended to replace both the straight-cut general service trousers worn by the Army as a whole, and also new issue of the *Berghose* to mountain troops. By now the old *Marchstiefel* high boot was rapidly being replaced with a less expensive ankle boot (*Schnürschuh*) and canvas anklets, so general service trousers designed to be gathered and secured at the ankle made sense. In practice, as always, much old stock was still seen in use many months after the introduction of the new pattern. The design differed from the *Berghose* mainly in being cut level at the waist, which was fitted with four long, downwards-buttoning belt loops. While buttons for attaching braces were still sewn inside the waistband, the use of a belt instead made it possible for the first time for a soldier to lower his trousers without first taking off his equipment and tunic – a real advantage under front-line conditions. Omitting the braces also made the use of shirtsleeve order when out of the line in hot weather much smarter. To save material and expense these trousers had no pocket flaps (except for one on the watch pocket), but the slash pockets were still fastened with buttons. The under-foot stirrups were retained, lacing at the outside vents.

(**Above**) These trousers are stamped with an RbNr and dated 1944. They are made from a superior smooth German tricot fabric; most examples were manufactured from standard *feldgrau* woollen materials.

NAMED GROUPS

Generalmajor Egbert Picker, 3. Gebirgs Division

The tunic displayed here belonged to Generalmajor Egbert Picker, formerly commanding officer of Gebirgsjäger Regiment 98 and briefly commanding general of 3. Gebirgs Division. (While his final rank was Generalleutnant, the tunic dates from his time as Generalmajor. To avoid confusion, throughout this 'Named Groups' section the rank headlined is that indicated on the collected uniform or document.) Picker was a veteran of World War I, during which he was awarded both 2nd and 1st Classes of the Iron Cross. He remained with the Reichswehr in the interwar years, and subsequently took part in the annexation of both Austria and Czechoslovakia. By the outbreak of World War II he was an Oberstleutnant (lieutenant-colonel), and his battalion took part in the invasion of Poland in September 1939. From late 1940 until early 1943 he was commander of Gebirgsjäger Regiment 98 in 1. Gebirgs Division, and in November 1941, in the rank of Oberst, he was awarded the Knight's Cross of the Iron Cross *(Ritterkreuz)* for operations with Army Group South in the Soviet Union. Colonel Picker was promoted to Generalmajor in July 1943, and for two short periods in August and September 1943 he filled in as interim commander of 3. Gebirgs-Division. He was further promoted Generalleutnant in mid April 1945, but went into captivity only three weeks later, remaining a prisoner of war until released in March 1947. He died in March 1960 in Ingolstadt, Bavaria.

Generalmajor Picker's tunic is typical of officer's-quality field service uniforms. As was often the case, it was made when Picker was a colonel and simply rebadged when he achieved general's rank. It is made of a high-grade *feldgrau* gabardine, with the conventional four box-pleated pockets, deep turn-up cuffs, and dark green stand-and-fall collar. All buttons are of gilt-washed pebbled finish.

(Left & below left) The collar patch design for all grades of general officer was the traditional *'alt-Larisch'* Arabesque used since 1900, in gold embroidery on *hochrot*. The embroidery sometimes incorporated several different types of thread; until 1939 gold bullion wire was used, but this was replaced with a yellow-gold thread called 'Cellon'. Picker's insignia are made from Cellon, but with gold wire central details to highlight the stylized leaves. The interwoven silver and gold wire shoulder boards show no sign of having received the gilt pip of General-leutnant during the three weeks he held that rank. The breast eagle is embroidered entirely from Cellon on a dark green base.

(Above) The sleeve badge is a high-quality hand-made example, with a border of silver bullion wire 'ropes'.

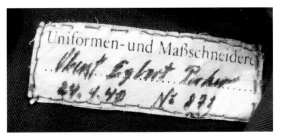

(Above left & left) The tailor's labels show that the tunic was made for Oberst Picker in April 1940 by C.W. Fischer of Nuremberg.

Hauptmann Robert Schöfer, Gebirgs Korps Nachrichten Abteilung 449

Robert Schöfer was commissioned on 1 January 1938 as a Leutnant in Gebirgs Nachrichten Abteilung 54 (Mountain Signals Battalion 54), the integral signals unit of 1. Gebirgs Division. In March that year he took part in the annexation of Austria, and was awarded the *Erinnerungs Medaille* on 13 March 1938. The 3. Kompanie of which he was an officer was the Gebirgs Funk Kompanie or 'mountain radio company' of the unit. At some date before mid 1942, Schöfer was transferred to Gebirgs Korps Nachrichten Abteilung 449, a signals unit under direct command of XVIII Gebirgs Korps, which included formations such as the 163. Infanterie Division, 7. Gebirgs-Division and 6. SS-Gebirgs Division 'Nord'. Schöfer served extensively in Lapland (northern Norway and Finland above the Arctic Circle), and his belongings include numerous maps of communications between units of the corps serving on this Murmansk sector of the Russian Front. After Finland made a seperate peace with the USSR in September 1944 all troops of the German 20. Gebirgs Armee had to withdraw, often under Finnish attack, into Norway, where they spent the remainder of the war. Robert Schöfer was awarded the Iron Cross 2nd and 1st Classes as well as the Long Service Medal, and on 1 November 1944 he was promoted Major. He survived the war.

This surviving tunic was perhaps made earlier in the war before Schöfer was transferred to the Lapland front. It is a tailored summer-weight garment, cut in the style of the service tunic but made from a hard-wearing sand-coloured cotton drill. Such tunics were popular with both officers and senior NCOs.

(Below) Also shown here is Schöfer's original *Erkennungsmarke* (identity tag) from his posting to 3. Kompanie, Gebirgs Nachrichten Abteilung 54. His blood group 'O' is stamped after the abbreviated unit designation. Note above and below the 'b' of 'Geb.' the low *Stammroll* (unit personnel roll) number '3', which shows that he was inducted when the unit was first created in October 1937.

Im Namen des Reichs

ernenne ich den Oberfähnrich

Robert S c h ö f e r

in der Gebirgs-Nachrichtenabteilung 54

mit Wirkung vom 1. Januar 1938 zum

L e u t n a n t

mit einem Rangdienstalter vom 1. Januar 1938 (1126).

Jch vollziehe diese Urkunde in der Erwartung, daß der Ernannte getreu seinem Diensteide seine Berufspflichten gewissenhaft erfüllt und das Vertrauen rechtfertigt, das ihm durch diese Ernennung bewiesen wird. Zugleich darf er des besonderen Schutzes des Führers und Reichskanzlers sicher sein.

Berlin, den 10. Januar 1938.

Namens des Führers und Reichskanzlers

Der Reichskriegsminister

Jn Vertretung

Keitel

(Above left) The insignia are the same as those worn on the field-grey tunics. Note the *zitronengelb* (lemon-yellow) Waffenfarbe highlights on the collar *Litzen,* identifying signals troops. The breast eagle is like that used on the *Waffenrock*, with a separate green wool backing.

(Above) As is common with these lightweight tunics, the interior lacks any lining. However, note the shoulder pads incorporated to give a better appearance, and the hemmed slot above the left skirt pocket for a sidearm hanger.

(Left) Schöfer's commission document as a Leutnant in January 1938. The seal on the lower left is actually impressed into the paper. This commission is signed by General der Artillerie Wilhelm Keitel, at that date Chief of the Wehrmacht Office.

Leutnant Helmut Diebel, Gebirgsjäger Regiment 100

Within the ranks of the Gebirgsjäger there were a cadre of highly qualified mountaineers, numbering just 380 officers and men. This elite group of Heeresbergführer or 'Army Mountain Leaders' included all ranks from NCOs up to the famous Generaloberst Eduard Dietl. One of these remarkably skilled soldiers was Oberfeldwebel, later Leutnant Helmut Diebel. Diebel entered the Army in 1935, and over the next five years he took part in the annexation of Austria and Czechoslovakia, and the invasions of Poland, the Low Countries and France. By the end of 1940 he had risen to the rank of Oberfeldwebel in 2. Kompanie, I Bataillon, Gebirgsjäger Regiment 100; he was a holder of the Iron Cross in both classes, and the Infantry Assault Badge (*Infanteriesturmabzeichen*); and he had joined the select band who had qualified as Heeresbergführer. The handsome badge marking this status was given on completion of the specialist training; its issue was recorded in the soldier's *Soldbuch* (paybook and abbreviated service record), and a log was kept to record the courses completed and the updating of the required skills. To keep the badge

the soldier had to refresh his status periodically, and he had to return it if his qualifications lapsed. (However, he could buy a personal copy from the manufacturer, at cost.) In 1941, Oberfeldwebel Diebel served in the invasion of Greece; and on 21 May the first elements of Gebirgsjäger Regiment 100 began to land under fire in Junkers Ju 52 transports on Maleme airfield, Crete, to support the hard-pressed German parachute and glider troops who had landed the previous day. Over the next few days Diebel and his comrades of I & II/GJR 100 were progressively landed on the island (the boats carrying III/GJR 100 were caught at sea by the Royal Navy, and that battalion almost ceased to exist). Helmut Diebel took his first wound in Crete, and in October he was awarded the Wound Badge in Black (*Verwundetenabzeichen in Schwarz*). Late in 1942 the commemorative cufftitle *'Kreta'* was instituted retrospectively for those who had fought in this very costly battle, and Diebel's award was dated on 31 December. By that time he was back in Germany, with the Wound Badge in Silver and only one leg.

Obefeldwebel Diebel on his wedding day, and the medals he wears in the photograph: Iron Cross 2nd Class, 4-Years Long Service, and medals for the Austrian and Czechoslovakian annexations. Also note in the photograph of the ceremony, on the chest of his *Waffenrock*, the pin-back Iron Cross 1st Class, Heeresbergführer badge and Infantry Assault Badge.

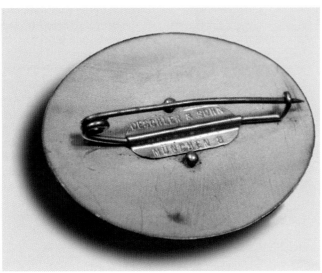

(Left & below left) The *Heeresbergführerabzeichen* or Army Mountain Leader's Badge is exceptionally rare, since most issue pieces were returned after the individual's qualification lapsed or he met his death. Shown here for the first time is Leutnant Diebel's personal badge, one of two he owned. This example is the issue piece, made by Deschler & Sohn of Munich. The oval badge is a vaulted brass plate 52mm x 42mm, with a white enamel band around the outside of the face bearing the title *'Heeresbergführer'* in black Gothic script. Inside this band is a Brunswick-green mottled enamel face, bearing a separately applied bi-metal edelweiss with no stem or leaves.

The stamens of the flower were applied as a separate piece, gold in colour, and the flower itself was then fixed to the badge with two dome-headed rivets. On the reverse is a brass 'safety pin'-style mount, which is held to the badge by a long metal plate bearing the name of the manufacturer, *'Deschler & Sohn München 9'*. The example shown is slightly broken: the wire hook normally loops back with two strands forming the catch. The second badge owned by Diebel was probably from the same manufacturer; it is identical apart from lacking the maker's name impressed in the mount.

(Right) Currently qualified Army mountain leaders, like the Heeresbergführer in this pre-war postcard photo, wore the badge on their left breast; but some period portrait photographs show it being worn on the right. This was the mark of a former recipient whose qualification had lapsed, so most such badges were presumably the privately purchased copies. However, after being severely wounded in Russia, Helmut Diebel was apparently allowed to retain the issued badge, simply switching it from his left to his right breast pocket – *see* tunic on page 66.

(Above) Helmut Diebel's actual Crete campaign cufftitle. It is 33mm wide, of white cotton with borders in golden-yellow 'Russia braid'. The title *'KRETA'* is embroidered centrally in the same colour, between two decorative palmate motifs recalling the capitals of ancient Greek temple columns.

(Left) The award document for Diebel's *Ärmelband KRETA*, in the name of GOC 12. Armee and signed by the regimental commander of GJR 100, Oberst Anton Glasl. It is dated 31 December 1942, and gives Diebel's rank as Leutnant. In fact his commission dated from 1 February 1943, but since he was then away from his unit and in hospital – and since hundreds of such documents were probably all presented to the colonel for signature in large batches – such a minor discrepancy is not significant.

(Below) Diebel's original 'dog tag', lying on the page of his *Soldbuch* on which the award of the *'Kreta'* cufftitle is recorded. The identity tag is marked for 'Gb. Jg. Ers. Batl. 100 2.Kp' – the Ersatz or replacement battalion for Diebel's regiment. Again, the low unit roll number '7' identifies him as a soldier of the first intake.

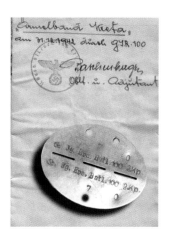

By early 1942 GJR 100 was heavily engaged with Army Group North on the Eastern Front, being committed to various sectors as a 'fire brigade' to count Soviet attacks. West of Leningrad in April 1942, Oberfeldwebel Diebel received a serious shell fragment wound to his left thigh. He was evacuated to the Reservelazarett (rear area general hospital) at Königsberg, East Prussia. Here infection set in, and eventually his left leg had to be amputated above the knee. Diebel spent four months in this hospital before being shipped back to Badenweiler in Germany – a reflection of the seriousness of his condition. After two months at Badenweiler he was transferred to the nearby military hospital in Freiburg, where he would remain for the next eight months as he made a slow recovery. During this time he was awarded the Wound Badge in Silver and, with effect from 1 February 1943, he was commissioned to the rank of Leutnant.

(Left) Diebel's paybook tells the story of his fourteen months in three different Reservelazarette hospitals. On 14 April 1942, presumably after initial treatment at a field hospital close to the front line, he was signed into the general hospital at Königsberg (Kaliningrad), on the Baltic coast behind the northern sector of the Russian Front. There his gangrenous left leg was amputated; he was shipped out on 19 August, and on the 26th arrived at Badenweiler in Germany. On 9 October he was moved to Freiburg, where he remained until 29 June 1943.

(Below left) Identification photograph of the newly commissioned Leutnant Diebel in 1943.

(Below) Gebirgsjäger medical personnel working in field conditions to try to save a similarly wounded soldier's leg.

On release from hospital at Freiburg, Leutnant Diebel was posted to Gebirgsjäger Ersatz Regiment 137 (Mountain Infantry Replacement Regiment 137) in Salzburg, most likely as a formality – his condition would preclude any duties other than administrative. The last entry in his *Soldbuch* places him with the same unit, but at Kufstein in the Austrian Tyrol. After this entry we have no further career information, but Replacement Regiment 137 was dissolved in June 1944. That summer the whole central Russian Front collapsed, and from then on it became common for Ersatz units to be transformed into combat units *en bloc*.

(**Above**) Among Diebel's effects was his service tunic as a Leutnant. This is the standard M36 type, in smooth tricot wool, with entirely conventional insignia. On the left forearm is the *'Kreta'* cufftitle, on the right upper sleeve the edelweiss badge.

(**Above**) On the right breast pocket there are thread attachment loops for the Heeresbergführer badge, worn in this position by former Army Mountain Leaders whose qualification had lapsed; there are photos of more than one Gebirgstruppe general wearing it in this way.

(**Right**) On the left breast is Diebel's award group. The four-place ribbon bar shows the medals for the annexations of Austria and Czechoslovakia, the Long Service Medal, and the Bulgarian Soldier's Cross for Bravery 2nd Class. Below this are a good quality vaulted Iron Cross 1st Class, the Infantry Assault Badge and the Wound Badge in Black. Diebel's Iron Cross 2nd Class and Wound Badge in Silver were not found among his effects.

Hauptwachtmeister Wilhelm Slunecko, Gebirgs Artillerie Regiment 111

This Austrian senior NCO held the artillery (and cavalry) rank equivalent to the infantry Hauptfeldwebel. Wilhelm Slunecko served at the start of the war in Gebirgs Artillerie Regiment 111 of 2. Gebirgs Division. Batteries of this unit served in Poland in 1939, in Norway and France in 1940, and in Russia from June 1941, when 2. Gebirgs Division was a formation of General Dietl's Gebirgs Korps Norwegen (later 20. Gebirgs Armee) on the arctic front. By mid 1942, however, the regiment was heavily engaged far to the south in the Crimea; and in May 1943

Hauptwachtmeister Slunecko was transferred with his Batterie to Gebirgs Artillerie Regiment 112 in 3. Gebirgs Division, then serving in the Southern Ukraine. In 1944–45 the unit fought on the retreat, back through the Carpathians, Hungary and Slovakia, and eventually surrendered in Silesia to Soviet forces. Slunecko survived the war and captivity, and was released from service in late March 1948 in Innsbruck. The set shown here consists of Slunecko's tunic, awards and award documents.

The tunic is a very fine example of an M36 garment upgraded for walking-out dress. The material is a high-grade *feldgrau* wool; the tunic was made in 1939, before shortages began to limit availability. A number of modifications have been made to improve its appearance. The bags have been removed from the lower pockets, which are sewn flat to the tunic. The collar has been enlarged, with more pronounced points in keeping with fashion. The adjustable cuff vents have been removed and deep turn-up cuffs added, as was permissible for a senior NCO. On these cuffs are the two bands of silver *Tresse* braid denoting the '*Spiess*' (literally, 'spear'). This was an appointment rather than a rank, but equivalent in function to battery sergeant-major, and the braid was only displayed while the soldier served in this capacity. His task as the senior non-commissioned soldier in the battery was to maintain the link between the officers and the lower ranks, which was an administrative job as well as a motivational one.

(Left) The shoulder straps have been sewn into the seams, and are probably originally from the *Waffenrock*. Note the thick cord piping in artillery *hochrot*, the white metal numerals and the pips denoting rank. Also seen here is a private purchase variant breast eagle, in white cotton embroidery on a mid-green wool. These appear to have been quite popular with NCO ranks early in the war.

(Right) Slunecko's decorations. On the left breast the ribbon bar shows awards of the Iron Cross 2nd Class; the *Kriegsverdienstkreuz* (War Merit Cross) 2nd Class with Swords; the *Ostmedaille,* for Russian service during winter 1941/42; a Long Service Medal; and the medal for the annexation of Czechoslovakia. On the pocket is the pin-back War Merit Cross 1st Class with Swords, above a Wound Badge in Black. On the upper left arm is the Crimea Shield, a campaign award to soldiers who fought in that sector between September 1941 and July 1942.

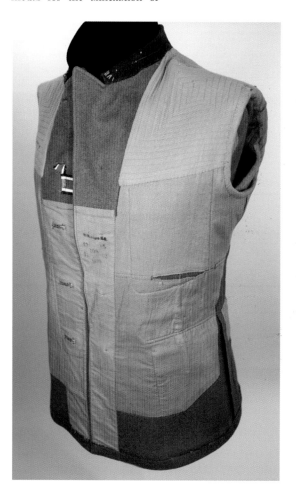

(Left) The interior of the tunic has had all extra pieces such as the medical dressing pocket removed to improve the appearance. The shoulders have been lightly padded, a feature found in many Austrian-made tunics. The depot stamp 'M39' for Munich, 1939, appears below the size and maker's markings.

IM NAMEN DES FÜHRERS
UND
OBERSTEN BEFEHLSHABERS
DER WEHRMACHT

IST DEM

Hauptwachtmeister Willi S l u n e c k o

8./ Geb.Art.Rgt. 111

AM 14. Juli 1942

DIE MEDAILLE
WINTERSCHLACHT IM OSTEN
1941/42
(OSTMEDAILLE)

VERLIEHEN WORDEN.

gez: von D a h m e n
Major u.Abt.Kdr.

FÜR DIE RICHTIGKEIT:

Hauptmann u. Batteriechef

(Left) Document for the award of the *Medaille Winterschlacht im Osten* or '*Ostmedaille*', on 14 July 1942. This award was also known to soldiers as the 'Order of the Frozen Meat', after their terribly harsh first winter in Russia, when the poorly equipped armies suffered heavy casualties from frostbite and exposure as well as to the major Red Army counter-offensive.

(Below) Hauptwachtmeister Slunecko's award document for the Iron Cross 2nd Class, dated 5 April 1943. Interestingly, the document is issued and stamped by the command of 320. Infanterie Division fighting outside Kharkov in the Southern Ukraine, to which Slunecko's battalion or regiment must have been temporarily attached. The signature is that of the divisional commander, General-alleutnant Georg Postel, a holder of the Knight's Cross with Oakleaves, who would die in Soviet captivity as late as 1953.

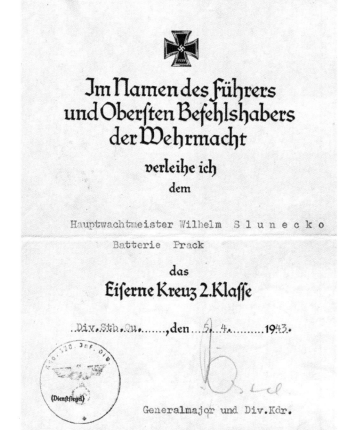

IM NAMEN DES FÜHRERS
VERLEIHE ICH
DEM
Hauptwachtmeister
Wilhelm Slunecko
11./Geb.Art.Rgt.112

DAS

KRIEGSVERDIENSTKREUZ
1. KLASSE
MIT SCHWERTERN

Div.Gef.St. , DEN 1. 9. 1944

(DIENSTSIEGEL)

(DIENSTGRAD UND DIENSTSTELLUNG)

Generalmajor u. Kdr.3.Geb.

(Left) Award document for the *Kriegsverdienstkreuz* 1st Class with Swords, dated 1 September 1944. Slunecko was now with 11. Batterie, Gebirgs Artillerie Regiment 112. The KvK 1st Class was the non-combat equivalent of the Iron Cross, and was probably awarded to Slunecko for exceptional organizational and administrative work. This document is signed by the commanding general of 3. Gebirgs Division, General-leutnant Paul Klatt, a holder of the Knight's Cross with Oakleaves.

Ritterkreuzträger Gefreiter Helmut Valtiner, Gebirgsjäger Regiment 143

An Austrian from the South Tyrol, Helmut Valtiner commenced his service in the Wehrmacht in December 1939. He took part in the invasion of France in 1940, and by 6 April 1941 he was a member of 1st Battalion, Gebirgsjäger Regiment 143 with 6. Gebirgs Division. On that date the German 12th Army crossed the frontiers from embattled Yugoslavia and Germany's Axis ally Bulgaria into north-eastern Greece, attacking Greek, British and Commonwealth forces amounting to eight weak divisions. By 18 April the Greek Metaxas Line had been breached, Salonika had fallen, and the Allies had been pushed south and west to a hasty defensive line on the Aliakmon River. On that day, I/GJR 143 was attempting to cross the Pinios Gorge against determined resistance from the New Zealand 21st Battalion and elements of Australian 6th Division.

When Valtiner's 1. Kompanie attempted a crossing they were driven back by heavy fire. Lance-Corporal Valtiner – who had recently been awarded the Iron Cross 1st Class – was leading a small Spähtrupp (scout group), and found himself out in front with just six other men. Pressing forward to ford the river in full equipment, Valtiner reached the far bank; there, despite being wounded, and separated from his comrades by artillery and machine-gun fire, he established a foothold that allowed his company to cross. The Gebirgsjäger then managed to outflank the Allied battalion, which was overrun; then continued their advance, capturing large fuel dumps and the port of Volos. Helmut Valtiner was evacuated first to Katarini, and then to a general hospital in Vienna.

Recommendations for high gallantry decorations had to pass right up the chain of command for scrutiny, from the soldier's battalion commander through regiment, division, army corps, army and army group, finally reaching the Oberkommando der Wehrmacht (joint services supreme command). Nevertheless, on 13 June 1941, Gefreiter Valtiner became the 305th recipient of the Knight's Cross of the Iron Cross – and only the second enlisted man in the German armed forces to be so honoured. Helmut Valtiner survived the war, and lived until 1987.

Knight's Cross presentation document *(Ritterkreuzurkunde)*

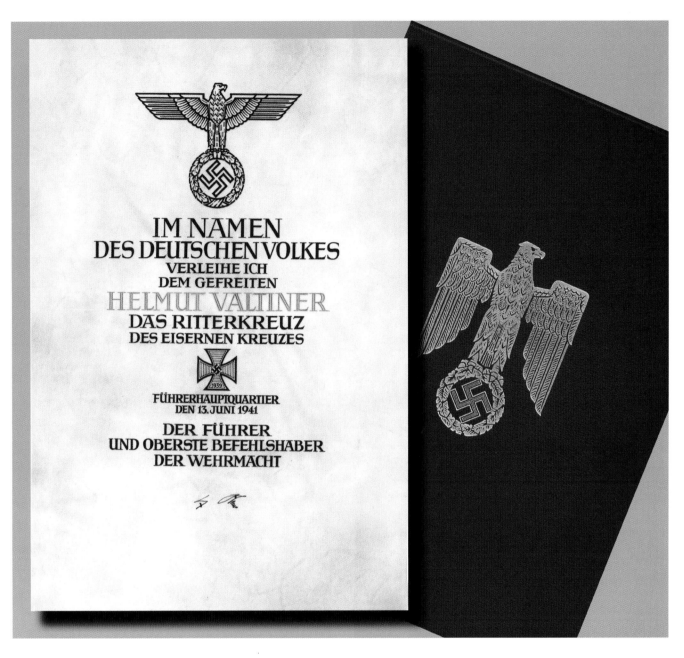

Shown here is the formal presentation document for Gefreiter Valtiner's Knight's Cross. These were sent directly to recipients' home addresses, some time after they had received – at the front or in hospital – the preliminary certificate of award *(Vorlaüfiges Besitzzeugnis)*, and had been physically decorated with the Cross by a senior officer. Documents of this quality were only presented until some time in 1942, with only a few specially favoured Ritterkreuzträger (Knight's Cross Bearers) receiving them thereafter. All elements of the impressive formal *Ritterkreuzurkunde* were hand-made by master craftsmen and craftswomen, and the increasing frequency of awards outstripped their ability to keep up with demand. Thereafter most recipients received only the preliminary certificate (*see* page 72). The 45cm × 36cm folder *(Mappe)* was covered in red Morocco kid leather, with 24-carat gold leaf border piping, and a large impressed gold eagle-and-swastika centred on the front. The name of the highly regarded bookbinder Frieda Thiersch, who made these folders, appears in gold at the inside bottom of the back panel. The document contained in the folder was executed on vellum parchment, imitating the finish of the smooth-scraped hide used for the finest medieval illuminated manuscripts. A large sheet of this parchment was folded in half to produce four sides; on the third side, below a hand-drawn national emblem, the text was executed by hand in dark brown ink by the calligrapher Franziska Kobell, with the recipient's name in 24-carat gold leaf. The inscription translates as 'In the Name/ of the German People/ I present to/ *(rank and name)*/ the Knight's Cross/ of the Iron Cross/ *(drawing of Knight's Cross)*/ Führer's Headquarters/ *(date)*/ The Führer/ and Supreme Commander/ of the Armed Forces'. Finally, Valtiner's document is personally signed by Adolf Hitler, whose tiny, crabbed script can be seen below the bottom line of the inscription. Some such documents bore a facsimile signature, and some went unsigned.

(Left) A picture from his own photo album showing Valtiner receiving the Knight's Cross in hospital from the senior medical officer, Generalarzt Zimmer. Valtiner would first have learned of the approval of his award from a brief congratulatory telegram.

(Below) Shortly after the first telegram, the soldier received the preliminary certificate (*Vorläufiges Besitzzeugnis*) confirming the award. These were pre-printed on stiff buff paper, 20cm × 14cm in size, with the details type-written. The signature is that of Generalfeldmarschall von Brauchitsch, at that date the German Army Chief of Staff (Oberbefehlshaber des Heeres).

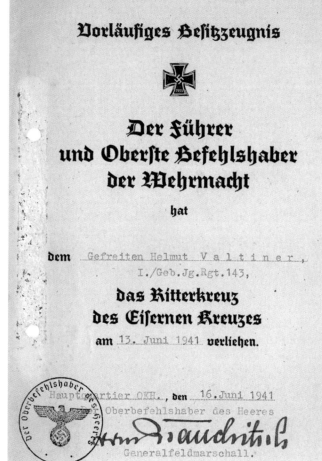

(Left) Outside the hospital in Vienna, Helmut Valtiner (centre) chats to several fellow patients, including two Fallschirmjäger. For some reason his replacement tunic does not display the chevron of Gefreiter's rank on the left sleeve. Note his *Berghose* tucked into his mountain boots. In the field short puttees would be wrapped around the ankle.

(Left) A commemorative portrait of Valtiner drawn by Parsch in 1941. The celebrated artist Wolf Willrich also produced a famous portrait sketch of him, which was widely distributed as a postcard.

(Below) Gefreiter Valtiner's award certificate for the Iron Cross 1st Class, dated just nine days before his historic action. The document is signed by Generalmajor Ferdinand Schörner as commanding general of 6. Gebirgs Division.

Im Namen

des

Führers

und Obersten Befehlshabers der Wehrmacht

verleihe ich

dem

Gefreiten Helmut Valtiner
1./Geb. Jäg. Rgt. 143

das

Eiserne Kreuz *1.* **Klasse**

Div. Gef. Stand, den 9. 4. 19 41

Schörner.

Generalmajor u. Div. Kdr.
(Dienstgrad und Dienststellung)

931 b Wehrkreisdruckerei XVII. A.K. Wien. 10.39.

(Left) While on leave, Valtiner is posed for a photo telling his story to young admirers. Note the *Bergmütze* on his knee.

Feldwebel Walter Waldegger, Gebirgsjäger Regiment 100

The story of Feldwebel Walter Waldegger is a testament to the amazing survival of some front-line soldiers in World War II. It has been the authors' pleasure to meet and speak with this remarkable man, but his kind of experiences were shared by many fellow soldiers of all the wartime armies.

Walter Waldegger finished his apprenticeship as a butcher at the age of 20, and was drafted into the Gebirgstruppe. After training with the 3rd Company of Mountain Light Infantry Replacement Regiment 137 in Glasenbach, outside Salzburg in Austria, he was posted to his combat unit Gebirgsjäger Regiment 100, in whose ranks he would serve throughout the war.

Greece

As part of General 'Papa' Ringel's 5. Gebirgs Division, in April 1941 GJR 100 took part in the invasion of Greece. They had what Walter recalls as a brutal baptism of fire in attacks against the Metaxas Line, a mass of defensive bunkers that were held with stubborn courage by units of the Greek 2nd Army; the Gebirgsjäger only broke through at great cost in lives. Shortly after victory in mainland Greece, the mountain soldiers of GJR 100 prepared for the next mission: the airborne assault on the island of Crete, defended by British, New Zealand, Australian and Greek

troops. Walter took off from Tatoi, Greece, on a Junkers Ju52 transport of KGrzbV 2 on 21 May 1941, the second day of the invasion. On crossing the Cretan coast they found that the airfield at Maleme was closed to further landings by the wrecks of many aircraft destroyed the previous day. Unable to land, the soldiers – who naturally had no parachutes – were forced to jump from the 'Aunt Judy' as it flew low over the sea along the edge of a beach at just above stalling speed, taking their chances on landing in water deep enough to cushion the impact but shallow enough not to drown them... Walter was lucky, but he describes this as a terrifying experience. The fighting that followed was extremely hard, as GJR 100 fought their way east and then south across the island, following the Allied rearguard all the way to the evacuation beach at Sfakion; it was an Austrian officer of the regiment who took the final Australian surrender on 1 June. Of some 22,000 men in total, the German attackers had nearly 6,500 casualties, of whom 3,350 were killed or missing. Once this costly battle had been won, Walter's regiment remained in occupation on Crete for a further six months, a time he describes as his best during the war, with plenty of free time to swim and sun-bathe. However, in late 1941 the regiment was transferred to Berchtesgaden in Bavaria, to acclimatize before its redeployment on the Eastern Front.

Russia

In that first dreadful winter in Russia, Walter found himself on the shores of Lake Ladoga south-east of besieged Leningrad, living in improvised earth-and-timber bunkers in temperatures of minus 38 degrees. He relates that at one point he did not remove his clothing, including boots, for three weeks on end. A sleeping bag was shared between three soldiers, who rotated in occupying it so that it was kept warm. The logistics broke down and the soldiers suffered badly from hunger as they fought off repeated Red Army attacks. The 5. Gebirgs Division remained on the northern sector of the Russian Front for another two years, until December 1943. In September 1942, during an attack on the Neva bridgehead, Walter was wounded by grenade splinters, and awarded the Iron Cross 2nd Class. The following year, at the battle of Mga in August 1943, he was wounded by shell fragments together with his Hauptmann Rosenberger; his friend Sanitäts Oberfeldwebel Franz Moser got both of them out of the front line. Walter had personally destroyed two Soviet tanks in close combat, by shoving Teller-mines with delay fuses onto the thinner hull top armour under the turret overhang; he received the Iron Cross 1st Class along with promotion to the rank of Oberjäger. After surviving several more close encounters with the Red Army, he was transferred with his regiment to Italy – where the weather in January 1944 was not dramatically better than in Russia.

Italy

Gebirgsjäger Regiment 100 took part in the battles for Cassino in the Gustav Line, being attacked by the

Walter Waldegger is shown holding his wartime and post-war awards. The medals and cross with ribbons folded into triangular shape are Austrian decorations.

Moroccans and Algerians of the Free French Corps just as they were taking over positions from 305. Infanterie Division on 12 January. General Ringel's division held out in bitter mountain fighting; they remained in the line – sometimes next to the Austrian 44. Infanterie Division 'Hoch und Deutschmeister' – until the Allied offensive in May pushed the defenders back up the Liri Valley, and the break-out from Anzio outflanked the whole Gustav Line. They kept fighting stubbornly back from ridge to ridge during Generalfeldmarschall Kesselring's carefully paced defensive campaign up the length of Italy. In July 1944 in the Abruzzi, Walter Waldegger was wounded for the fifth time. During that year he also attended the Heereshoch-gebirgsschule (Army High Mountain Troops School) at Fulpmes in the Tyrol, completing four of the five courses required to become a Heeresbergführer. Despite not being officially recognized in this specialist role, he was employed as a Heeresbergführer for the rest of the war.

The Alps
On 2 October 1944 the now-Feldwebel Waldegger took part as a squad leader in a legendary operation against French Chasseurs Alpins on Mont Blanc, Europe's highest

peak. A small team from II/GJR 100 set out to climb the Italian side of the mountain in a howling blizzard, finally reaching the Torino rescue hut (at an altitude of just under 11,000 feet – 3320m) at 3am the next morning. The hut was held by about twenty French mountain soldiers, but nobody had imagined that a climb in such conditions was possible, so it was badly guarded. Waldegger and his comrades attacked with grenades, capturing the hut and twelve prisoners and inflicting three killed and four wounded. Walter took charge of the squad that led the prisoners down the Italian side of Mont Blanc, after an extraordinary feat of stamina, mountaineering and skill-at-arms. Walter's unit was later transferred to the Little St Bernard Pass, where on 8 April 1945 he suffered his seventh wound, again from shrapnel. He was still in hospital when Germany surrendered a month later, passing into American captivity but being released on medical grounds in August 1945. Since the war Walter Waldegger has been a respected figure in his local community in the Tyrol. He has been a border control police commander, and also a builder of some of the major chair-lifts in his region. At the time of writing he is still alive.

(Right) Feldwebel Walter Waldegger's *Soldbuch*. Here we see the identification photo, rank upgrades, and details from his identity tag (below). His *Erkennungsmarke* is stamped for his original unit, 3. Kompanie, Gebirgsjäger Ersatz Regiment 137, with the unit Stammroll number '1509'.

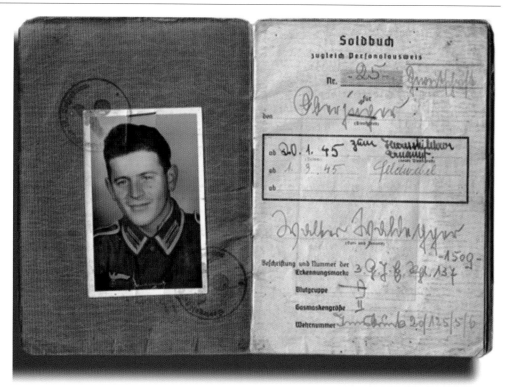

(Right) Pages 21 and 22 of the paybook, listing awards. From the top of page 21 they are: Wound Badge in Black (14 September 1942); Iron Cross 2nd Class (1 October 1942); Wound Badge in Silver (6 August 1943); Iron Cross 1st Class (17 August 1943); and Infantry Assault Badge (10 September 1943). Opposite, on page 22, are entries for the Wound Badge in Gold (1 September 1944) and Close Combat Clasp in Bronze (1 February 1945).

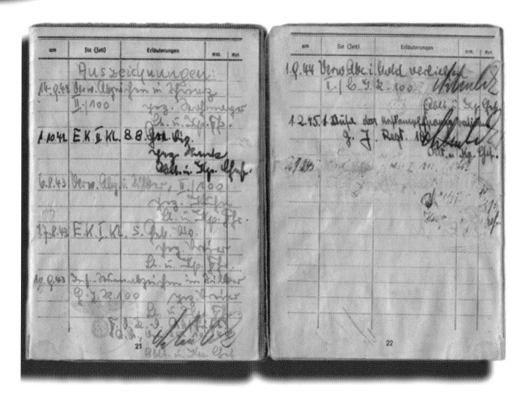

BESITZZEUGNIS

DEM

Obergefreiten Walter Waldegger
(NAME, DIENSTGRAD)

8.Kompanie/Geb.Jäg.Rgt.100
(TRUPPENTEIL, DIENSTSTELLE)

IST AUF GRUND

SEINER AM ___3. 8. 1943___ ERLITTENEN

3 MALIGEN VERWUNDUNG – BESCHÄDIGUNG

DAS

VERWUNDETENABZEICHEN

IN ___Silber___

VERLIEHEN WORDEN.

Btl.Gef.Stand .DEN 6. 8. 19⁴³
J.A.

(UNTERSCHRIFT)

Hauptmann u.Btl.Kommandeur
(DIENSTGRAD UND DIENSTSTELLE)

II./Geb. Jäg. Rgt. 100

(Left) Award certificate for the *Verwundetenabzeichen in Silber,* given after Walter was wounded at Mga near Leningrad, by fragments. Details of a wound were not entered on this document, but may be found in some paybooks if they required hospitalization. (Note, in such cases, that the German for hand grenade is *handgranat,* but *granat* unqualified means 'shell'.) The date on this *Besitzzeugnis* – 3 August 1943 – and the date the award was entered into his paybook are a few days apart, as was normal. The certificate is signed by the captain then commanding II/GJR 100.

(Right) His fifth wound, in Italy, brought Walter the Wound Badge in Gold on 16 July 1944; the paybook entry for this was not made until 1 September. II Bataillon now had a new commanding officer, Major Johann Zwickenpflug.

BESITZZEUGNIS

DEM

Oberjäger Walter Waldegger
(NAME, DIENSTGRAD)

8./G.J.R.100
(TRUPPENTEIL, DIENSTSTELLE)

IST AUF GRUND

SEINER AM 16.7.44 ERLITTENEN

5 MALIGEN VERWUNDUNG ODER BESCHAEDI-
GUNG DAS

VERWUNDETENABZEICHEN

IN ___Gold___

VERLIEHEN WORDEN.

O.U. , DEN 1. 9. 19 44
J.A.

(UNTERSCHRIFT)
Major II./G.J.R. 100
(DIENSTGRAD UND DIENSTSTELLE)

(Left) Snapped wearing a camouflaged helmet and the mountain *Windjacke,* Walter's comrade throughout five years of war, the medic Sanitäts Oberfeldwebel Franz Moser, who rescued Walter and Hauptmann Rosenberger when they were both wounded at Mga in north Russia. Their friendship continued for many years after the war.

(Above) Walter Waldegger's photo album includes this atmospheric snapshot of his exhausted squad in combat just 3 miles (5km) from Leningrad. He recalls that from this place they could see one of the tank factories in the city; after they called up an 8.8cm flak gun and destroyed several tanks the Soviets would only bring them out after dark. Note the soldier in the centre, cradling one of the rare 7.62mm Walther G41 semi-automatic rifles.

(Right) In this late war photo taken in Italy, Unteroffizier Waldegger wears his favourite bleached field cap, the ribbon of his Iron Cross 2nd Class in his button-hole, the pin-back Iron Cross 1st Class, Infantry Assault badge and Wound Badge in Gold.

Gefreiter Heinrich Eckkramer, Gebirgsjäger Regiment 138

In 1939 Heinrich Eckkramer, from Salzburg, Austria, joined Gebirgsjäger Regiment 138, a unit of Generalmajor Eduard Dietl's 3. Gebirgs Division. He received standard infantry training, and went on to further instruction as a field medic with Gebirgs Sanitäts Ersatz Abteilung 18. In March 1940 he was made a Gefreiter, and shortly afterwards GJR 138 sailed off to war, heading for Trondheim in Norway. On 9 April 1940 German troops invaded Norway by sea and air, landing to seize ports all the way from Kristiansand in the south to Narvik in the north – the latter, the objective of the rest of 3. Gebirgs Division. On 16–18 April, British and French expeditionary forces landed at Namsos north of Trondheim and Aandalesnes south of it. Eckkramer's unit was entrusted with defending Steinkjer at the northern end of Trondheim Fjord, and were successful after a bitter four-day battle. The regiment then pushed north to relieve their hard-pressed comrades in Narvik, where 6,000 Germans were resisting 20,000 British, French, Free Poles and Norwegians. Several companies, including Eckkramer's 3. Kompanie, I. Bataillon, were flown into Narvik. The Allied situation changed dramatically when news came of the German Blitzkrieg into the Low Countries and France from 10 May onwards. Although Narvik fell on the 28th, the German force managed to retreat eastwards, and the Allies began to evacuate their units from the north on 3 June. Norway finally capitulated on 10 June 1940.

In June 1941, GJR 138 was sent to the Finnish border above the Arctic Circle, to attack towards the vital Soviet port of Murmansk. This offensive bogged down in the summer swamps – harder to cross than the winter snows; Eckkramer was wounded by a hand grenade during a final unsuccessful push in September. In May 1942 he was promoted to Sanitäts Obergefreiter. On 27 November he was wounded yet again, taking shell fragments in the shoulder, during the attempt to prevent the encirclement of the important rail hub of Velikiye Luki on the Lovat river. On that very day the encirclement was completed by four Red Army Guard divisions. On 7 December 1942, Eckkramer suffered a gunshot wound during the defence of the unit's encircled pocket south of the city. This was partially relieved in early January 1943, but totally lost on 16 January; casualties were so high that Eckkrammer was lucky to survive. His wounds seem to have made him unfit for front line duty until June 1944, when he was transferred out of the Mountain Troops and into Grenadier Regiment 53. In August 1944 he was back in action on the Eastern Front, and was wounded yet again, receiving the Wound Badge in Silver. He also won the Iron Cross in both classes, the Narvik Shield and the Infantry Assault Badge. Heinrich Eckkramer survived the war, but was apparently much troubled by his wounds in later life.

(**Right**) Eckkramer's album contains extremely rare photos of the improvised airlift that carried elements of his regiment nearly 400 miles (600km) to Narvik after the successful defence of Trondheim. On 8 May 1940 the 2., 3. and half of 6. Kompanie of I./ and II./GJR 138 were flown north, in Eckkramer's case aboard one of only six Dornier Do 26 seaplanes ever built. On 25 May two of them, including this one, were caught unloading supplies at Rombaksfjord by three Hurricane fighters of No.46 Sqn RAF, and were destroyed on the water.

(**Left**) Men of Eckkramer's 3. Kompanie loading their gear aboard the Do 26 that will fly them to Narvik; the seaplane airlifted an officer and thirty-six men of the company that day. At left, note the Kriegsmarine sailor manning the boat, and at right a Lufwaffe officer with an Oberleutnant's rank patch on the sleeve of his flight suit – thus making this one the rare photos to show men of all three services of the Wehrmacht together in a combat zone.

(**Right**) Gefreiter Eckkramer's Narvik campaign shield and the award document. Just under 8,600 shields were presented to soldiers, sailors and airmen who took part in the battle between 9 May and 9 June 1940. The shields for Army and Air Force were in white metal, that for the Navy in yellow metal; the cloth backing patch was in the appropriate colour of the service uniform – field-grey, grey-blue or dark blue. The document is signed by General der Gebirgstruppe Dietl, commander of 3. Gebirgs Division and the Narvik Group; note that it is dated only on 10 November 1940.

(Left) In the Eckkramer album is this photo of two Gebirgsjäger in greatcoats, contemplating the field grave of a Fallschirmjäger Gefreiter. This paratrooper now lies in the main German war cemetery in Narvik.

(Below) Gefreiter Eckkramer took this informal snapshot of Generalleutnant Dietl with his men outside his HQ at Bjørnfjell in May 1940. This humble stone railway worker's cottage was built in the early 1900s, and still stands to this day. The defence of Narvik made Dietl's reputation as one of the Wehrmacht's early war heroes.

(Below) Eckkramer's *Erkennungsmarke,* with its leather pouch, pierced like the tag to sling round the neck; soldiers often made or purchased these in various materials, to keep the metal tag off the skin. The tag is marked to 3. Kompanie, Gebirgsjäger Regiment 138; Eckkramer's blood group is '0' and his unit roll number '236'. He wore this tag throughout the war.

'Demoted' Unteroffizier Johann Perr, formerly Gebirgs Artillerie Regiment 118

Johann Perr has been left until last in this section, since his surviving documents tell an interesting story of a 'disciplined' soldier. Perr joined 3. Batterie of Gebirgs Artillerie Regiment 79 in 1937, at the age of 22. Gunner Perr appears to have done well at first, being awarded the artillery lanyard for excellent shooting (**below right**) in October 1938, and being promoted to Gefreiter (lance-bombardier). He served with this regiment of 1. Gebirgs Division in Poland, before being transferred to Gebirgs Artillerie Regiment 118 in 6. Gebirgs Division, going on to serve in France, Greece, and then on the Lapland front in Finland and north Russia. In June 1941 he was convicted of galloping his horse without permission, and for this trivial display of high spirits he was confined to barracks for

seven days. Despite this misdemeanour he was promoted Unteroffizier (equivalent to senior corporal or lance-sergeant) in December 1941. In April 1942, just a week before a major Soviet offensive, Perr was severely wounded by a shell fragment in the forehead; this seems to have consigned him to home service with replacement units for the rest of the war. In November 1942, while serving with 5th Company of Mountain Artillery Replacement and Training Regiment 112, he was convicted of attempted theft and sentenced to six weeks in cells and demotion to the ranks. In July 1944 his rank was finally reinstated, but an unsavoury mark remains on his surviving *Soldbuch*. The front cover (**below left**) carries a red line slashed across it, with the word *degradiert* ('degraded', literally 'demoted').

(Right) All soldiers' records were kept in a central file called a *Wehrstammbuch* (military record book). This was a complete dossier on everything related to a soldier's service, including units served in, awards, where he was employed, medical records and disciplinary proceedings. The pages **(below)** titled *Strafen* (punishments) record Perr's transgressions. The central column on the upper page records his seven days' confinement for misuse of his horse.

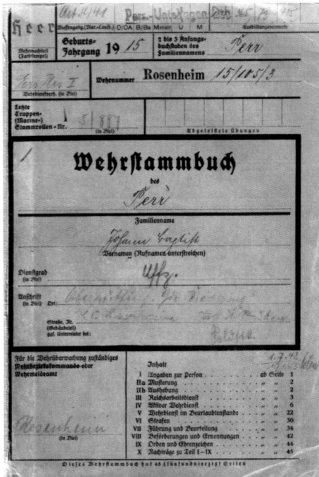

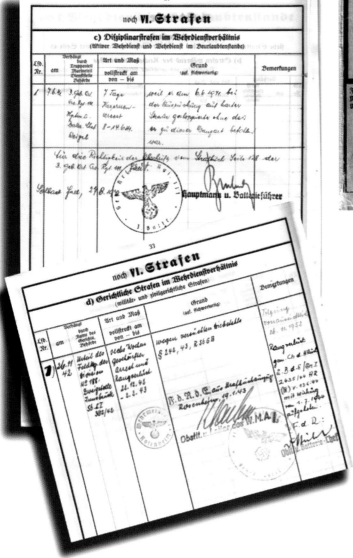

(Left) The lower page records Perr's sentence of six weeks imprisonment and reduction to the ranks for the offence of attempted theft. Such crimes were taken extremely seriously in the Wehrmacht, and were usually punished severely.

PROTECTIVE CLOTHING

Footwear

The provision of special clothing and equipment for the Gebirgsjäger was obviously important in light of the environments in which they were intended to operate and the special demands of their mission. They were required to carry out operations in exceptionally rugged terrain, sometimes in conditions of snow, ice and high winds, and often far from regular bases and supply lines. Thus they had to carry with them much of their necessary equipment not just for combat but also for subsistence – weapons, munitions, climbing equipment, rations and medical supplies. In the mountain environment a great deal of self-sufficiency was demanded, from the unit level down to the individual soldier. The special equipment started with one

of the Gebirgsjäger's most basic but important tools: his feet. The mountain boots or *Bergschuhe* provided for both climbing and skiing, and also protected the feet in harsh terrain. These boots, made from thick brown leather, were ankle height for ease of movement and for wear with anklet gaiters or cloth puttees, and the tops had an edging of field-grey cloth to prevent chafing. The boots generally laced up at the front through seven pairs of eyelets; however, some examples have been observed with eyelets at the bottom and lacing hooks above. This appears to be a simple manufacturing variation, although quite a few climbing items procured from civilian sources were almost identical.

(**Right & below**) The unique sole had a rhomboid pattern of small cone-shaped studs in the centre, repeated smaller on the heel. Around the edges of the heel and the sole were a number of steel cleats, to protect the boots from the abrasion of rock surfaces and to aid climbing. On either side of the toe there were a pair of special cleats with flat faces, to fit inside the toecap of the binding when wearing skis. For the same reason, the heel was grooved to retain the rear spring fastener of the ski binding in use at that date.

(**Left**) The stacked leather heel of the *Bergschuh,* grooved to accomodate the rear spring of the ski bindings. Note the boot's strong construction, with a heel cap and a sealing strip running up the rear spine. The leather is thick and of a good quality. The outer faces of the steel cleats are also seen; these had a long nail underneath and were hammered into the boot, with the lobed outer face protecting the outside edges of the heel and sole. The exceptionally hard abrasion that is unavoidable during rock-work can quickly damage conventional boots.

(**Right**) The soft field-grey wool edging around the ankle opening to prevent chafing; this was a consistent feature of issue mountain boots. Note also, just visible inside the ankle, the issue numbers impressed into the leather lining. These are sometimes found repeated on the outside in the corresponding place, or on the leather inner sole. The size was usually impressed into the underside of the instep of the sole.

(**Left**) Note the different appearance of the pair of cleats on the side of the sole level with the toe, which have flat outer surfaces so as to fit securely into the forward ski binding. The other cleats have a wider, shallower shape with a lobed centre for grip on rock. Earlier boots sometimes had flat brass plates.

The mountain troops were also supplied with climbing shoes (as opposed to boots) called *Kletterschuhe*. These soft shoes were usually worn during climbing training and practice, but although not generally intended for demanding field work they were carried on operations for the most difficult rock climbs. The *Kletterschuh* had something of the appearance of a moccasin, being a grey canvas ankle-length shoe with a soft brown leather outer shell covering the heel, sides and vamp. The leather was sewn in two panels, one around the front of the shoe and the other around the rear. There were seven pairs of lacing eyelets down the front, and black or white laces were used. The sole was made of a flexible thick felt with no heel or instep, which allowed the wearer to get grip on a rock face. There was also an almost identical type referred to as *Hüttenschuhe* ('hut shoes'), which differed only in having leather rather than felt soles. These were intended for wear in mountain huts or where the heavy, hobnailed *Bergschuhe* were otherwise inappropriate.

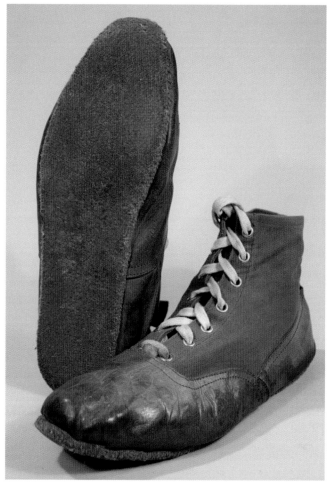

(Left) The *Kletterschuhe* being worn by Gebirgstruppen under instruction in roping techniques for an Army Mountain Leader course.

(Below) These later-pattern *Kletterschuhe* are made entirely of camel-coloured suede, with six pairs of lace holes.

(Left & below) The mountain boots were generally worn with short puttees – *Wickelgemaschen*. These long strips of elasticated woollen cloth, wrapped around the ankle to seal the top of the boot against snow and give extra support, were made in a variety of grey and grey-green shades. They came in three lengths – long, medium and short. The longest were general Army issue from before the war, to be worn up to the knee with the early Reichswehr breeches; the shorter puttees were specifically for Gebirgsjäger, and were usually maker-marked with a variety of woven labels.

(Right) The puttees ended in a long, narrow tape, which was passed through a metal friction buckle to tighten and secure the seal. A small hook marked 'L' or 'R' (for *links* or *rechts*, left or right) was often fixed to the inside end of the puttee, so the winding process started with the cloth firmly anchored to the boot.

(Left) During the war a version of the general issue canvas anklet gaiters was produced for the Gebirgstruppe. These differed from the universal type in having leather reinforcing strips around the edges. They too often have a small hook inside the bottom edge, like that which secured the cloth puttees to the boot. In practice these gaiters were rarely seen, and the cloth puttees were used until the end of the war.

(Left & above) A high canvas spat-type gaiter was also issued, which came above the ankle and covered the whole top part of the boot. Commonly referred to as the 'Styrian gaiter', after a region of Austria, this was made from a stiff olive-drab canvas with heavier reinforcing strips at the edges. It laced down the outside through a series of hooks, with lace holes at top and bottom and a heavy canvas base strap with a friction buckle. An iron wire stirrup with a ring at each end passed under the instep; the rings were retained by another heavy strap with a friction buckle, which passed back across the top of the foot and through a canvas loop sewn to the front of the gaiter. Occasionally the stirrup is also found in webbing instead of wire. Note the metal tips to both straps, which are often maker-stamped. This example of the gaiter carries the RbNr that dates it to after 1942, and the marking *'Große II'* – Size 2 (medium).

(**Right**) The mountain boot retained in the binding of a military ski, the rear spring gripping tight in the bevel of the heel. Note the metal cheeks of the forward binding seat, which make clear why the front pairs of sole cleats had to have flat outer faces.

(**Left**) Snowshoes were also issued to Gebirgsjäger when necessary. The oval wooden frame was laced with a pattern of rope retaining a canvas panel, which provided support on the soft surface. A series of crude canvas straps were laced through metal rings to keep the boot firmly in place.

Wind jacket *(Windjacke)*

One item issued exclusively to the Gebirgsjäger in view of their special requirements was the wind jacket. This was a double-breasted protective overjacket, worn by all ranks from private to general, and was as synonymous with the Gebirgsjäger as the *Bergmütze* itself. The jacket was made from a waterproof cotton duck in an olive-green colour, and was cut generously enough to fit over the belt equipment. It reached to the thigh, and closed with two rows of five buttons down the front, of which four were usually visible. These buttons were either grey horn, grey-green glass or concave metal 'washer' type. The large fall collar had a hook-and-eye for securing the closure at the throat. Underneath the leading edge of the collar there was a tab-and-button arrangement to allow the turned-up collar to be secured across the chin. There were two box-pleated pockets on the skirt, and two slanted vertical 'muff' (hand-warmer) pockets in the lower chest. These all had scalloped flaps secured with single buttons. The cuffs had a buttoning tab with two tightening buttons, and the back of the jacket was provided with a half-belt that secured with two buttons, across a long, open pleat down the back that allowed for some size expansion.

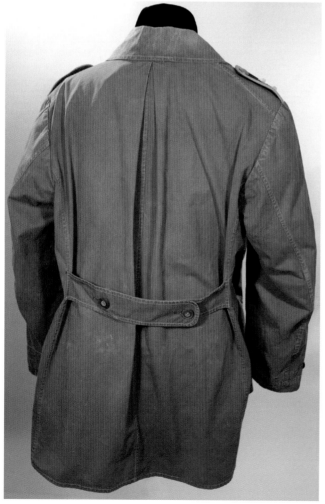

(Left) The shoulders were provided with a cloth bridle and button for wearing slip-on shoulder straps, but this Oberfeldwebel chose to sew the straps permanently into the shoulder seams. Note the very pale 'meadow-green' shade of this Waffenfarbe piping. Many soldiers also ignored regulations and sewed the edelweiss badge to the upper right sleeve.

(**Left**) Proof of the popularity of the *Windjacke* with all ranks: General der Gebirgstruppe Rudolf Konrad wears his – and a rucksack – during operations in the Caucasus Mountains of the southern USSR in 1942. Apart from the flash of colour from his red, gold and silver shoulder boards, from 20 yards away the general could be mistaken for any trooper.

(**Left below**) The maker's stamp identifies Schaal & Saulter of Reutlingen, a town on the edge of the Black Forest just south of Stuttgart. The depot stamp is 'M39' for Munich, 1939. Note the usual size stamps: '43' (upper left) is the length of the back to the waist, '88' (lower left) is the overall length, '49' (upper right) the collar size, '67' (lower right) the sleeve length, and '96' (centre) the chest size.

(**Below**) The fabric colour has faded with hard wear, but was originally an olive-drab shade. The excellent construction of the jacket can be seen here; note the strong double seams of the side and skirt pockets. The two-button cuff closure allowed tightening for a better seal against bad weather; here one of the large horn buttons was replaced during wartime with a similar but not identical type.

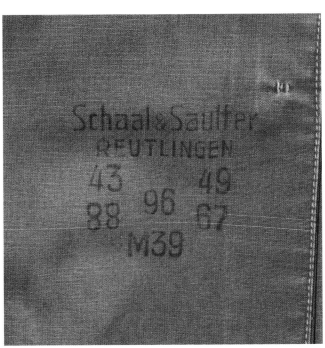

Snow camouflage wind blouse *(Windbluse)*

Several types of winter camouflage clothing existed, some of which were exclusive issue to the Gebirgstruppe. Others became general issue, as the German forces found themselves engaged in winter environments on several fronts. The first article, introduced in 1938 specifically for the Mountain Troops, was a white show-camouflage wind blouse; this was the forerunner of the general issue anorak. The *Windbluse* was a large, loose, thigh-length oversmock of pull-over construction, with an integral hood; it was intended for wearing over all uniforms and equipment.

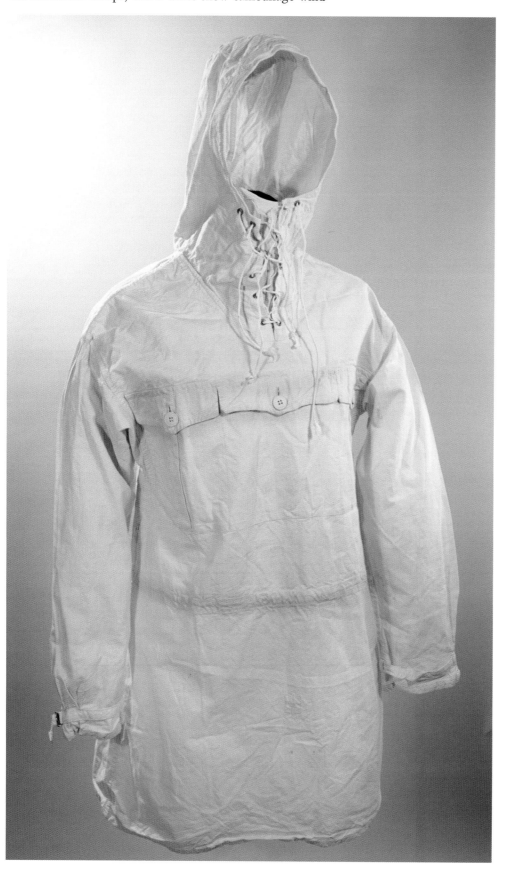

The smock had three patch pockets on the chest, with reverse bellows pleats in the outer two, and scalloped pocket flaps closed with white plastic or painted horn buttons. Variants have been observed with only two pockets, and also with normal box pleats. From the throat to the base of the hood there were a set of five pairs of white-painted eyelets for a tightening and loosening lace – this was necessary because the smock was pulled on and off over the head. A further single eyelet each side of the base of the hood took a drawstring for the hood itself. Behind this front laced opening there was a sealing panel to prevent drafts. There was a drawstring in an internal 'tunnel' around the waist; and each cuff had a fastening tape with a friction buckle, to seal the cloth around the wrist (examples with large buttons instead of buckles are also occasionaly seen). While the smock was naturally intended to be worn without insignia, several period photos show soldiers with a breast eagle sewn to the right breast or the upper left sleeve, but this was a personal and non-regulation touch. Production of this garment ceased at some time in 1941, probably in anticipation of the production of the reversible smock and trousers, which in fact did not reach the front until 1942.

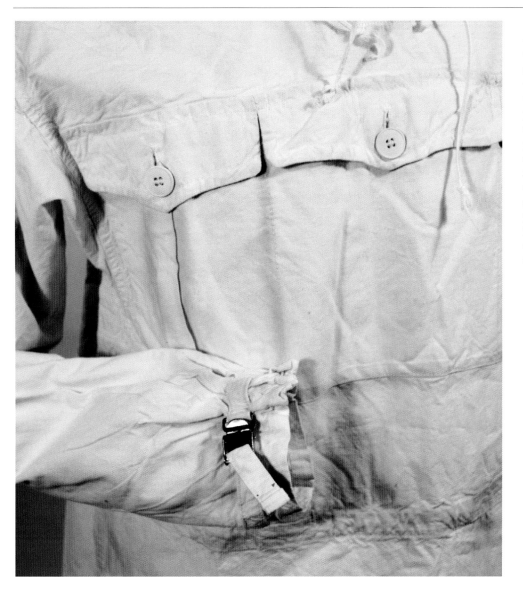

(Left) The fabric is a tightly woven cotton duck; this is water-repellent, but some examples show repeat treatment as the protection was lost. Note the three patch pockets in a row across the chest, the large central one plain and the two slightly narrower flanking ones having reverse pleats to allow for expansion. Each pocket is secured by a large white plastic button. The friction buckles on the cuff tapes of this example are chrome finished.

(Below) The opening upper chest panel and the neck and hood are a separately-made assembly from the body of the smock, and are double-stitched for insulation. The weatherproof quality is also improved by a fly flap on the inside that covers the laced opening from the rear. Note the zinc eyelets, most of which have lost their original white celluloid coating.

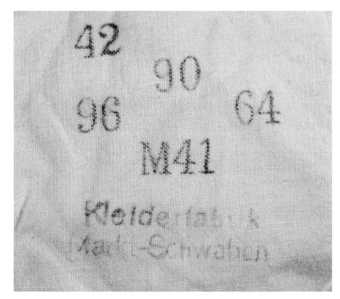

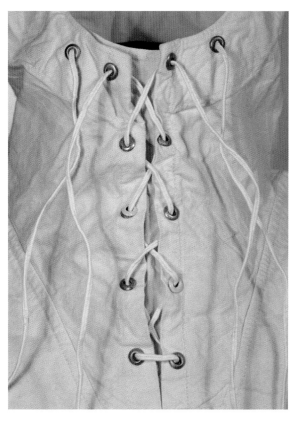

(Above) The interior stamping shows the usual size measurements, but omits the upper right numerals – a collar size was redundant on this article. It is further marked 'Kleiderfabrik Markt-Schwaben', having been made in the province of Schwabia south of Munich. The depot stamp is 'M41' for Munich, 1941; this is therefore likely to be an example of the last of these Windblusen issued.

Reversible camouflage anorak

Introduced in 1942, the new reversible camouflage anorak superseded the plain white *Windbluse*. (The term anorak is used here to differentiate it, but it was clearly a direct development of the all-white smock, and its design showed only minor improvements.) Its success with the Gebirgsjäger led to its subsequent issue to many other types of frontline troops fighting in winter conditions.

Similar but not identical in construction to the wind blouse, it was made now from a windproof cotton duck fabric that was white on one side and grey-brown on the other; it was therefore completely reversible, and could be used in snow conditions and periods of thaw, when the Russian mud was notorious.

Again, it was a pullover smock, cut large to fit over the uniform and belt equipment. The front closed with five pairs of lacing eyelets, with a single pair above this for a hood drawstring. On both white and grey-brown sides of the front vent there was a permanently fixed fly panel that closed across the neck with three buttons, thus completely covering the laced opening. The buttons were generally of pressed paper, as on this example. There were again three patch pockets across the chest, the outer two being pleated and all having scalloped single-button flaps; but there was also an internal pocket in each rear hip with an external buttoning flap. The internal waist drawstring was unchanged; but there was now a slit centred low in the rear, and a button low on the front, which allowed a long cloth strap to be passed under the crutch and fastened at the front to hold the skirt down snugly; this could be used with either the white or grey-brown sides outermost. The cuff straps, fitted with friction buckles, were now held in place by several bridle loops. On the front and back of each sleeve just below armpit level there was a button, for the attachment of a coloured identification band – since Soviet troops also wore white clothing, this field sign was a sort of visual password. Arm-band colours and combi-nations were changed regularly, for obvious reaons of security.

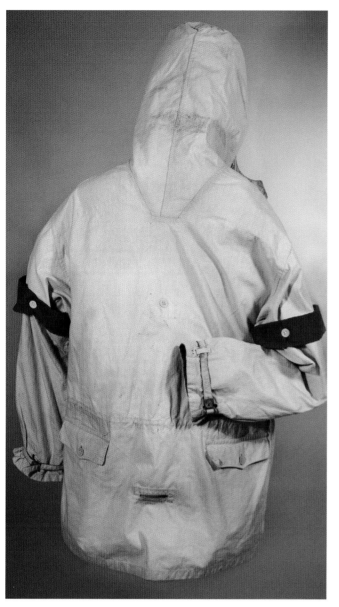

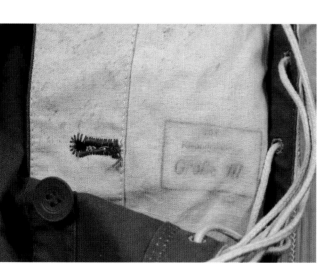

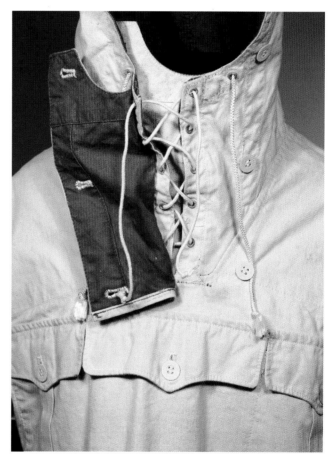

(Left) This rear view shows the two back pockets, and the rear of the hood, which was cut large enough to fit over the steel helmet. The long cuff tapes, with grey zinc friction buckles, are held in place by several cloth bridle loops. Note the slot for the crotch strap; mounted inside, this could be passed through the slot when the other side was exposed. The identification armbands buttoned to the sleeves are original period pieces.

(Above) The hood and the opening for the head were again sewn as a separate piece from the body of the smock, double-stitched for strength and weatherproofing. Note the buttoning fly flap across the lace-up vent; there was a separate flap on each side of this reversible garment.

(Above) This example is faintly marked on the white side of the front fly cover. It is date-stamped, and the word 'Kleiderfabrik' can be made out below, above the size 'Größe III' – Size 3, large. Note the pressed paper button, and the colour of the drab side of the fabric. The exact shade could vary from this brown, through olive-drab, to grey.

Reversible camoufage trousers

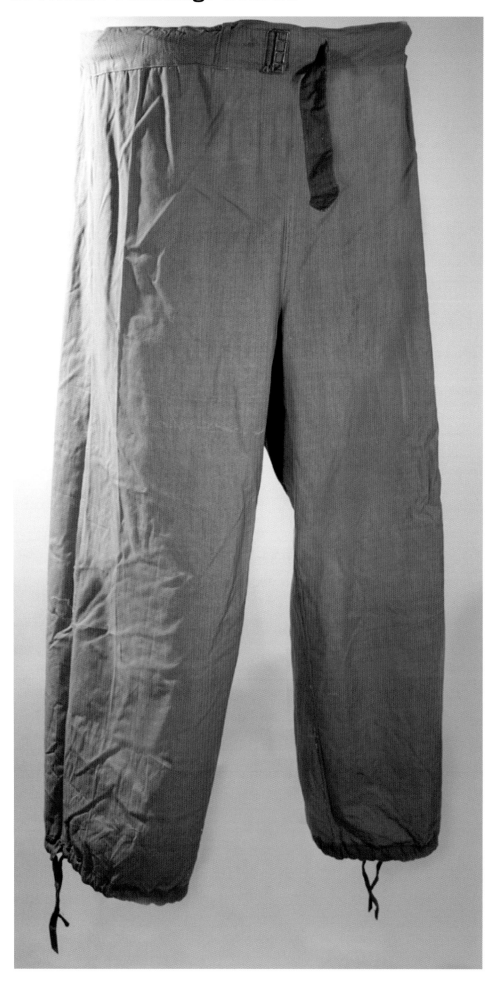

The new anorak introduced in 1942 was issued together with a matching pair of reversible camouflage over-trousers, of a voluminous and shapeless cut. These were made from the same windproof and water-repellent fabric as the smock, white on one side and brown or grey on the other. They had a simple internal cloth waist-belt with a three-pronged buckle for tightening, and an internal tie string at the bottom of each leg. These over-trousers were not particularly popular with the troops, partly because of their large, flapping size and partly because they were made without pockets, so that the wearer had no access to the pockets of his service uniform worn underneath.

Details of the cloth internal waistbelt, and the tie-tapes at the base of each leg.

Snow camouflage smock

This garment superficially resembles the snow camouflage wind blouse, but can readily be distinguished in photos by its through-buttoned front and the absence of chest pockets. Like the wind blouse, these snow smocks were originally intended only for Mountain Troops, but became much more widely used when it was realized that the war in the Soviet Union – envisaged as being a short conflict – was going to grind on for years. Some early Gebirgsjäger examples had a very loose-fitting back to allow for wear over the rucksack, but generally these smocks were of a simple single-breasted overcoat design that reached to the knees. A large hood to accommodate the helmet was provided, and there were drawstrings or buttoning tabs at the cuffs. This example also has two open patch pockets at the hips, and a wide cloth drawtape for the hood.

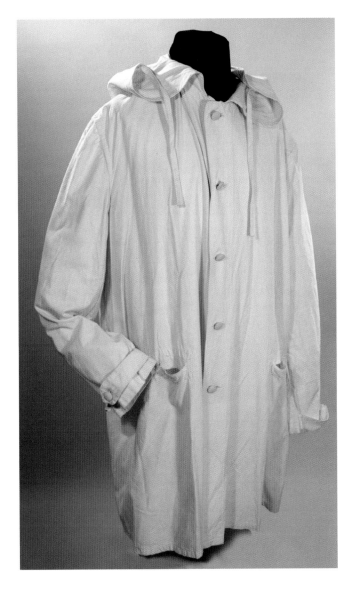

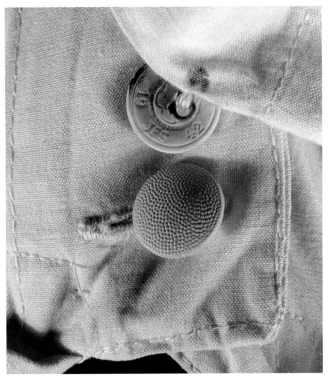

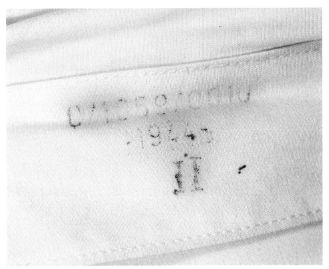

(Top) It is interesting to note that while the buttons appear to be painted metal they are in fact made of cast resin, right down to the manufacturer's mark and date ('JFS 1942').

(Above) This example also carries an RbNr, the date '1944', and a size mark 'II'.

EQUIPMENT

Ski equipment

An integral part of the Mountain Troops' mission was the ability to use skis. There was an issue model of skis, but these were supplemented, especially later in the war, by an increasing number of civilian models donated by the German public in the winter donation drives. (These appeals did not bring in only cold-weather clothing, but anything else that might be of help in the Russian winter, for which the government and the Wehrmacht high command had so notoriously failed to equip the troops in winter 1941/42.) The issue pattern skis were painted white with a broad green stripe down the centre of the top; the base was cut square, unlike the rounded bottom surface of civilian skis. The Wehrmacht used a variety of bindings manufactured by a number of different firms; to confirm their approval these were stamped by the Waffenamt (Ordnance Bureau), as were the wooden skis themselves. The bindings had a metal base on which the boot sat, its raised cheeks having an adjustable gap for different boot widths. A buckled leather strap retained the toe of the boot, and a metal spring at the rear clamped into the groove above its heel. Ski poles were made from a wooden or bamboo shaft with a leather grip binding and wrist strap at the top, and a metal ferrule at the end. Above this an open wooden ring was retained around the shaft by four web or leather straps, allowing this base to angle freely on the surface of the snow.

Ski equipment

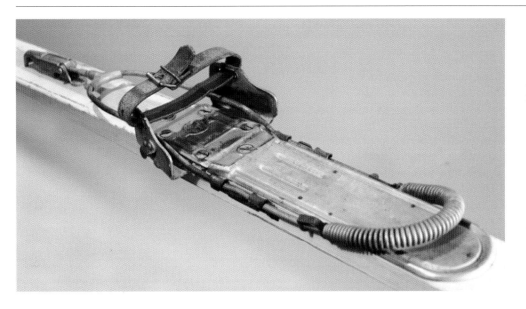

(Left) The bindings are seen here from three-quarter rear; note also the square-cut side and bottom surfaces of the military ski. The clamp at the front was raised to release the spring loop at the rear; the skier then placed his boot on the metal plate and inserted the toe between the cheeks and under the leather strap, and clipped the spring around the grooved boot-heel. He then pressed the front clamp down, to tension the heel binding.

(Right) These skis are marked underneath the tips by the maker, Heinrich Hammer of Ulm, and display the Waffen-amt approval stamp. A serial number was also often stamped into the top surface.

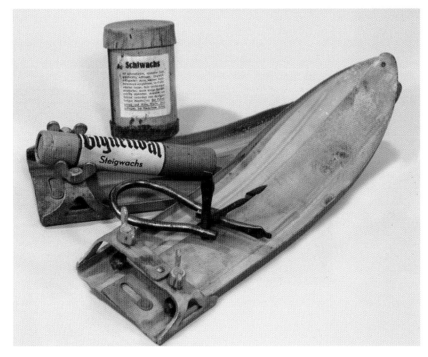

(Left) A small canvas bag of accessories was usually supplied along with the skis. These included self-clamping ski tips in case of breakage, a folding multi-tool for making adjustments or repairs, and even spare binding plates and heel springs. Two period containers of ski-wax are also shown here.

Climbing equipment

An essential piece of equipment for climbing was the ice pick *(Eispickel)*, used for breaking ice, removing loose rock and providing leverage when climbing steep inclines. They consisted of a steel head on a wooden shaft, with a square-section steel spike protruding from a ferrule. Around the handle, retained by a metal stud low on the tapering shaft, was a movable ring with a tough webbing wrist strap, generally in olive-drab or natural off-white with a pair of fine red stripes. The most famous manufacturer was the company Stubai, who also made items such as pitons and crampons. Apart from their maker's mark picks were usually stamped by the Waffenamt on the head and/or the handle.

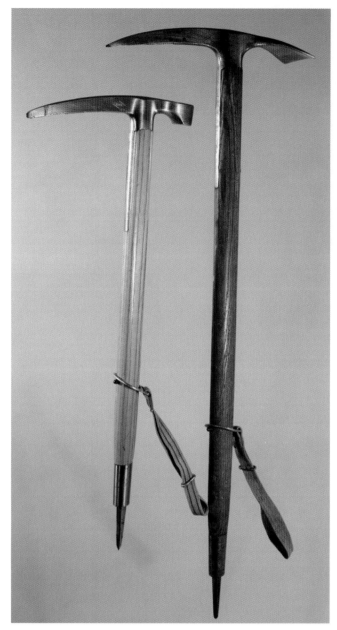

(**Right & below**) Two types of pick bearing the diamond-shaped Stubai maker's mark, the longer one with a mattock-type blade and the shorter with a hammer head for driving pitons. Both types came with a leather protective cover (**bottom**). The longer pick illustrated is stamped on the shaft to 'GJR 137' (**bottom right**); quantities of climbing gear were abandoned by this regiment when 2. Gebirgs Division left Norway in late 1944 after retreating from Finland, and have subsequently appeared on the collectors' market after being disposed of by the Norwegian Home Guard.

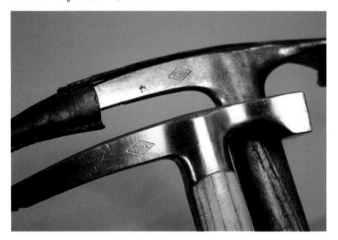

(Right) All the hardware needed for climbing and roping had to be carried with the soldier; it was issued as required, and then returned to stores. Shown here are: Two ice hammers *(Eishammer)*, one marked 'GJR137' on the handle; note the varying shapes of the heads, although their purpose is the same. Several Italian-issue and many civilian items found their way into German use. Pitons, for horizontal (left) and vertical cracks (right), the former on an original *karabiner*. Ice pins (centre) had long screw heads for anchoring ropes to ice.

(Left) Three original examples of the several types of ropes issued; from top to bottom, red rope for avalanche rescues, the general issue rope with green flecking, and plain rope. A list of the equipment required by a two-man rope team for a difficult climb was listed in one manual as follows: 1 mountaineering rope (10mm × 40m), 1 climbing [piton] hammer, 3 pitons for horizontal cracks, 1 piton for vertical cracks 1 ring piton, 1 wafer piton, 4 karabiners, 2 pairs of climbing shoes, 2 long cord slings (5mm × 2.5m), 1 short cord sling (5mm × 1.5m), 2 first-aid packets, 1 small backpack, 1 prismatic compass, map and guide, 1 electric flashlight, 1 altimeter.

(Right) Crampons were strap-on spikes for ice climbing. The larger ones, as used by the Hoch-Gebirgsjäger, came in 10- and 12-spike size for the entire foot; the smaller four-spike version was for the front sole only. They were retained by a single canvas strap laced through metal rings on the sides, and a metal toe strap. A canvas bag with a metal protective plate in the base was provided for carrying the larger crampons.

Rucksack, Model 1931

The mountain troops' rucksack was constructed of waterproof olive-drab canvas. It consisted of a large central sack with a rectangular top flap secured by three buckled leather straps; this central compartment had a drawstring closure through metal grommet eyelets. At the base was a large rectangular pouch with a two-strap top flap, and on each side, placed close to the back, was a further deep vertical pocket with a single-strap flap; all flaps were edged with leather reinforcing strips. Two pairs of leather loops for stowage straps were sewn to the top flap to retain the mess kit, and a further three loops – one on the top and one each side – enabled the rolled greatcoat to be strapped on.

(Below) The leather carrying straps were retained by two large metal rings attached to the upper rear of the pack by a leather panel. The straps were adjustable for length; they passed over the shoulders and down, to attach to 'D'-rings on the belt cartridge pouches by flat grey-painted metal hooks. Behind the centre of each carrying strap there was a further 'D'-ring retained by a leather tab, which connected under the armpits to a pair of straps mounted at the bottom rear corners of the pack. These bottom straps each had an adjustable carbine hook; when clipped to the 'D'-rings behind the carrying straps these secured the pack tightly. An additional waist strap could be attached to stop the pack swaying, which was important when skiing or climbing.

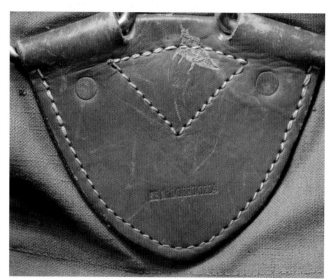

(Above) This example carries the RbNr on the rear leather panel; earlier pieces often show manufacturer and date marks.

Sleeping bag (*Schlafsack*)

A rarely seen item is the 'sleeping bag for high mountain infantry' *(Schlafsack fur Hoch-Gebirgsjäger)*. A revolutionary design for its time, this was later used as the model for the post-war Bundeswehr's sleeping bags.

The bag covers the full length of the body and has a hood to cover the head. It is made of brown-grey waterproof cotton on the outside, and has a green lining on the inside. This lining incorporates numerous cotton pockets filled with down-feathers, and can be unbuttoned in panels for airing, refilling or cleaning. The outer cover into which the sleeping bag is rolled for carriage closes with a series of large buttoning flaps, and is an integral part of the bag, forming the area covering the feet. A clever feature of the design is a zipper running along the top of this bottom section; it can be removed, effectively leaving the wearer with a long, down-insulated coat. Down both the upper sides of the bag a long zip-fastened slash covered with a fly flap allows the wearer to remain in the bag while having his arms outside. The front is fitted with a button-ing patch pocket either side. The front closure also fastens with a long zipper (all are Zipp brand), covered with a buttoning fly panel. At the top of this fly a buttoning tab closes it across the throat. Above this is the hood, with a three-button fly panel closure much like that on the reversible anorak, which protects the lower face. The Gebirgsjäger veteran Walter Waldegger told the authors that he once spent three months near Lake Ladoga in northern Russia more or less living in this type of bag, not removing his clothes or his boots for three weeks.

Mountain equipment accessories

(Right) Each soldier was issued with four olive-drab cotton bags for stowing equipment, and two boot bags. Most had metal grommets with drawstrings around the top; the equipment bags had triangular panels in various colours at the corner, so that those holding various items of gear could easily be identified from one another. Also seen here is a field-made bag for a small stove as used by some troops. The stove runs on petrol, and came with various accessories such as a spanner tool and filling spout. The assembly was closed with a screw lid, and when opened three angled bars were turned outwards to support a mess tin for heating.

(Left) A Gebirgsjäger, wearing the reversible anorak, settles down in his snow cave. A small climbing stove (probably a civilian item) heats a mess tin; and at right, note one of the many styles of Army-issue lanterns, hanging from a suitably placed entrenching tool.

(**Right**) At top, a pair of waterproof olive-drab calico over-mittens, the thumb and the area opposite it reinforced with leather. Note the wrist strap with a friction tightening buckle, and a loop and toggle to secure the gloves together for carrying. Below left are grey suede leather gloves typically worn by officers, but available for private purchase by enlisted personnel. Below right are a pair of general issue grey woollen gloves; the white rings round the folded cuff indicate sizes – from one, up to four for extra large. At bottom left are a pair of issue wristlets *(Pulswärmer)*; despite being officially discontinued in 1937 these were seen in use throughout the war.

(**Below**) At top, slotted snow goggles *(Schneebrille)* which protected the eyes from bright direct and reflected sunlight. Examples also exist with white wool and rubber bodies supporting the carefully designed metal vision plates. The second pair are heavily tinted and have mesh sides to protect the eyes from rock splinters; the lower two pairs are simply tinted for sun protection – note small ventilation holes around the rims of the lenses, to prevent condensation.

Pack-horse equipment

While every Gebirgsjäger could find himself carrying approximately 70lbs (32kg) of equipment, much had to be carried by the pack-animals which virtually replaced wheeled transport in mountain terrain. The steadfast friend of the Gebirgsjäger was the 'Muli' – a popular term in fact used for both mules and tough little Haflinger horses. In addition to their heavy harness the mules could transport 220lb (100kg) loads, and the horses 176lbs (80kg), up to the highest alpine positions – a task impossible for any man. All branches of the Gebirgstruppe relied on these animals to complete their missions and bring up supplies. Artillery pieces including the 7.5cm Gebirgsgeschutz 36 (M1936 mountain gun), which weighed 1654lbs (750kg), could be broken down into eight animal-loads, with a further five mules being required to lift 40 rounds of ammunition. A mountain battery consisted of four such guns, with sixty-eight mules and 175 men. Signals cables were also laid from a special drum that attached to the pack-saddle; engineers used pack-animals to transport equipment such as bridging items and mechanical saws, and they kept the mountain infantry supplied with food and ammunition. It was a partnership of which all Gebirgsjäger were proud, but men and animals serving side by side were often pushed to the limit of their endurance – *see* also the photo on page 125.

(Right) The foundation for all loads was this M23 carry-saddle *(Tragegestell)*. An iron frame adjustable to the animal's size has left and right pads, of leather covering stuffed canvas, which rest on the folded blanket on the animal's back. The frame has iron hooks, clamps and rings for attachment to the leather harness and to accept various loads. General loads were carried in wicker panniers *(Tragekörbe)*; these had a pair of triangular iron rings at the back for hanging the load from the saddle hooks (visible at the tops of the wide side struts). Loads not carried in special containers were rested on horizontal fold-out metal frames and plates (here seen folded up, between the side struts). This leather harness is original; note the broad webbing surcingle, and the small pouch for spare horse-shoes strapped to the top board.

(Left) Special items, such as artillery and small arms ammunition and medical equipment, came in their own purpose-built cases – even insulated metal containers for hot food could be attached to pack-saddles. Here a horse is used to lay field telephone cable for a Gebirgs Nachrichten signals unit, with a backpack cable-laying drum clamped to the top of the carry saddle.

(Right) The medical equipment and supplies of a Gebirgs Sanitäts Kompanie were set up at unit level for pack transport in various configurations, for everything from triaging wounded at a forward aid post to carrying out operations at a surgical station behind the front line. Anything from dressings to surgical instrument sets, oxygen, sterilizing and anaesthetic equipment, even folding operating tables were packed in wicker panniers and metal cases. There were four types of cases (Gebirgs Sanitäts Kasten) for the most commonly used instruments, dressings, ointments and tablets, clearly marked with their contents for immediate recognition. The photo shows a case numbered '3' and marked 'Binden' and 'Flüssigkeiten' (dressings, and liquids); stretcher-bearer and Red Cross armbands; a tunic with the medical specialist forearm badge; a pannier; and a medical pack with a ponyhide flap.

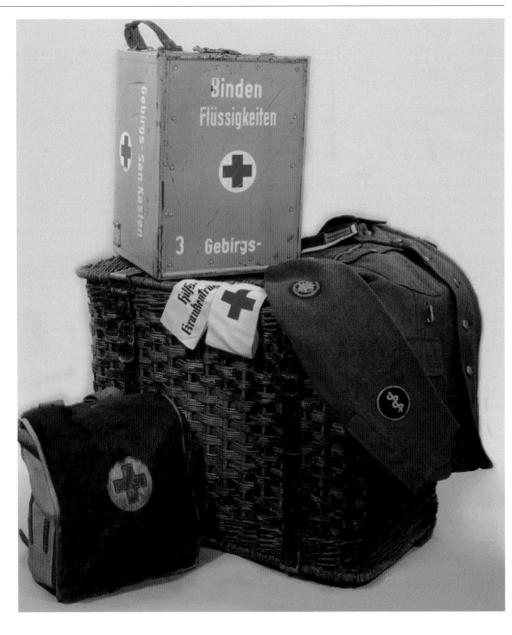

(Left) General Ludwig Kübler of 1. Gebirgs Division watches a mule train pass, with wicker panniers on the front mule and large unit medical cases packed on the following animal. (Kübler was executed in 1947 for warcrimes during his anti-partisan operations in Yugoslavia.)

Identity tags

Every serviceman of the Wehrmacht was required to wear an *Erkennungsmarke* (identity tag). These tags were worn around the neck at all times, and were made of thin sheet aluminium in an oval shape measuring approximately 7cm × 5cm. The tag had three horizontal slots cut across the centre, and the wearer's abbreviated details were recorded identically on the upper and lower portions. In the event of the soldier's death the tag was broken across the perforations, one half remaining on the body and the other being passed back to the unit for a record to be made of the

casualty. Two holes were punched near the top edge and one at the bottom for carrying the tag on a string; strings often got broken and were replaced with any suitable kind of lace or cord. German tags differed from Allied 'dog tags' in that they did not bear the wearer's name, for security reasons. They recorded his first unit – often a replacement regiment or battalion – in abbreviated form, with the man's number on that unit's nominal roll (*Stammroll*), and his blood group (*Blutgruppe*). Tags could be replaced to reflect a later unit during the soldier's subsequent career.

(Right) At left is a tag to '*3./Gebjäg.Ers.Rgt 139*' – 3rd Company, Mountain Light Infantry Replacement Regiment 139. A man's first posting was normally to his assigned combat unit's Ersatz regiment or battalion, a pool of replacements to be posted forward as needed. Since large numbers of men passed successively through such holding units, the soldier's personal number on the unit roll was often high – here, '5223'. His blood group 'O' is scratched on rather than stamped.

The right-hand tag is stamped '*4./G.J.R. 137*' for 4th Company, Mountain Light Infantry Regiment 137, with the low unit roll number '43' indicating a soldier of the original intake, and blood group 'A'.

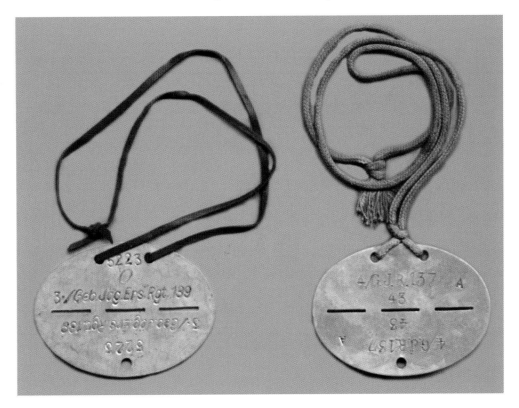

(Left) The left tag here is for 5. Kompanie, GJR 99, with the roll number '191'; the blood group 'O' has been mistakenly stamped twice at the bottom. Each Gebirgsjäger regiment had three battalions each of about 900 men. Each battalion had three rifle companies, the 4th being an infantry gun company, with 2 × 7.5cm guns, a mortar platoon and a machine gun platoon; battalion HQ also had signals and combat engineer platoons. Companies were numbered in sequence right through the regiment, so e.g. the gun company of II Bataillon was 8. Kompanie.

The right-hand tag is for 3. Kompanie, Gebirgs Sanitäts Ersatz Abteilung 18 (Mountain Medical Replacement Battalion 18), with the roll number '520' and blood group 'AB'.

MISCELLANEOUS ITEMS

Regimental flags

In March 1936 new flags and standards were bestowed on the regiments of the Army by the Supreme Commander, Adolf Hitler. The universal design created by the artist Paul Casberg reflected in general layout that of Prussian regimental flags since the days of Frederick the Great in the 18th century, but with modern charges. On a ground of the appropriate Waffenfarbe colour, it showed in natural colours a Wehrmacht eagle with wings turned downwards and clutching an unwreathed swastika in its talons, the whole surrounded by an oakleaf wreath, and superimposed over the centre of a large Iron Cross; a mobile swastika was displayed in each corner.

These new *Fahnen* were magnificent works of art, hand made by teams of highly skilled artisans; the design was intricately hand-embroidered in metallic and fine wool threads on a single piece of ribbed silk mounted on a stretcher frame, with a separate team working on each side. The design on the obverse (as shown here) was directly replicated on the other side, so that on the reverse (i.e. when seen with the staff to the right) it appeared in mirror image. The *Fahne* measured 125cm square, with bullion fringes on three sides. It was mounted on a varnished oakwood pole with silvered fittings, surmounted by a silvered finial showing a cut-out Wehrmacht eagle in a voided spearhead – also designed by Casberg. A silver brocade streamer with edge-stripes in national colours was attached below the finial; other streamers were also designed to honour those units that had taken part in the annexations of Austria, the Sudetenland and Memel, but in the event these were never presented. The flags were unidentified except by the regimental unit title on an engraved silver collar around the shaft below the silk. Battalions had smaller swallow-tailed guidons of identical design.

(Right) An unissued BeVo-quality example of the sleeve badge for a Gebirgsjäger Fahnenträger (flag-bearer), introduced in August 1936 for wear on the right upper arm of the service and parade tunics, and later extended to the greatcoat, by the senior NCOs honoured with this regimental appointment. The shield-shaped badge was folded underneath before sewing to the uniform.

1. Gebirgs Division *Edelweissring*

At some time in 1942 a tradition was established of awarding an edelweiss ring to deserving men who made some worthy contribution to their units. This award was recorded in the *Soldbuch,* and a document was given to the recipient, although presentation was strictly unofficial and sanctioned only at divisional level.

(Left) The document recording the presentation of the ring in March 1944 to Gefreiter Johann Krammer of Gebirgsjäger Feldersatz Bataillon 79.

(Below) The upper ring is one of the 'presentation' pieces, made of either silver or silvered brass; the area behind the oval head is vaulted, not solid. The middle one is a private purchase ring, with a slightly smaller head; it is made from silver.

(Bottom) The privately made ring is stamped inside the band with '800' for the silver content; the solid back is engraved in italic script *'1.Geb.Div. 1.3. 1944'.*

20. Gebirgs Armee *Lapplandschild*

Another unofficial award appeared at the very end of the war, above the Arctic Circle. The formations and units of 20th Mountain Army had been forced back out of Finnish Lapland into northern Norway following the conclusion of a separate peace between the USSR and Finland in September 1944. At some date before the 280,000 German forces in Norway surrendered to the British (by radio) on 7 May 1945 their commander, General der Gebirgstruppe Franz Böhme, ordered the institution of a 'Lapland'

campaign shield to honour his men. Official approval for the *Lapplandschild* was not given before the surrender of Germany, but the award was subsequently produced in local factories and award documents were distributed. The actual shield comes in many more or less crude forms, being stamped, cast, and even hand-made. The document also comes in various formats; it is always dated after VE Day, and does not feature the swastika. The award was also retrospectively recorded in the *Soldbuch*.

Note that the document named to Feldwebel Paul Rosenleitner of 9. Kompanie, Gebirgsjäger Regiment 139 uses that regiment's honorary title *'Generaloberst Dietl'*, which was bestowed on it following Dietl's death in June 1944. The document is dated as late as 12 July 1945, at Jordamo in Norway, and is signed by the major commanding GJR 139 in captivity. The thin, crudely made shield bears a map of Lapland, surmounted by a Wehrmacht eagle but without a swastika.

Training

Specialist training in mountain warfare techniques was naturally a priority in the Gebirgstruppe. Soldiers of all ranks and units had to master specialized techniques and methods of climbing, cross-country movement, combat, and survival in snow and mountainous terrain. This required very 'hands on' methods of training and practice, based on instruction manuals such as those seen here. Various schools were established to teach skiing, high-altitude climbing and winter operational techniques for infantry and mountain artillery, and there was even a separate mountain troops' medical school.

The photos shown here were taken at the Army High Mountain School (Heereshoch-gebirgsschule) at Fulpmes in the Austrian Tyrol. Here, specialist skills in high mountain climbing, survival and combat were taught to a select number of Gebirgsjäger.

In addition to the divisional regiments, four separate battalions designated Hochgebirgsjäger Bataillonen were formed. Two Skijäger Regimenter were also raised, and formed the nucleus of a division on the central Russian Front in summer 1944.

Souvenirs and commemorative items

Souvenirs were produced for sale to families and other civilians to honour soldiers, and for soldiers to buy as a reflection of pride in their service. They range from the hand-made to the mass-produced; this small selection of examples shows, **clockwise from top left:**

Brass ashtray commemorating service in 2. Gebirgs Division, 1942–43; hand-painted wooden platter for wartime Christmas (*Kriegs-Weihnacht*) 1942 at Bad Reichenhall with 4th Company, Mountain Signals Training Battalion 18; metal paperweight cartoon silhouette of a Gebirgsjäger; Christmas 1942 brass plaque from the *Eismeer Front* (literally 'ice sea' – the Arctic Circle); Christmas 1939 beer stein for 1. Kompanie, Gebirgs Träger Bataillon 56 (Mountain Pack Battalion); and a service remembrance stein for 3. Kompanie, GJR 100.

(Below) Illustrated postcards were popular, with colour or monochrome artwork or photographs.

(Left) Despite the serious nature of their employment, Gebirgsjäger were young men like those of any Army, and often made light of their situation with the help of soldiers' humour. This small book of cartoons from 1. Kompanie, Gebirgsjäger Regiment 98, reveals a little of how they saw themselves. It was not the soul of wit, but it was cheerful, and that was all they asked.

„Esel — prima, sag i dir! Den Bauch a bißl unterstütz'n und an ‚Austeilschutz' hinten, dös ersetzt an Muli."

(Left) A striking portrait of an Unteroffizier of a Gebirgs Panzerjäger Abteilung, detailed down to the rose-pink highlights of anti-tank troops on his collar *Litzen* and *Schulterklappen*.

(Below) Dated 1940, this pastel of an Oberfeldwebel of Gebirgsjäger was perhaps drawn by a talented comrade.

(Left) Local pride: this postcard portrays a sturdy mountain infantryman from Sonthofener, the most southerly town in Germany. It lies in a Bavarian valley surrounded by popular climbing locations – the obvious home for a Gebirgsjäger.

(**Right**) A painted postcard showing a Scharfschütze (marksman) as he takes aim. Apart from the *Bergmütze*, the edelweiss flower in the bottom left corner underlines the Mountain Troops identity.

(**Left**) This sketch dated 1942 shows Oberleutnant (here Hautpmann) Rieger from GJR 137, who led one detachment of volunteers from his unit in a parachute jump to relieve the defenders of Narvik. Note his *Narvikschild,* and – below his Iron Cross 1st Class, Infantry Assault Badge and Wound Badge – the Fallschirmjäger parachute qualification badge.

(**Right**) Another piece of ephemera with a shooting connection: a large poster confirming that 2nd Prize in a shooting contest from the 1943 officer's training course in Salzburg was won by Leutnant Rudolf Ernst of Gebirgsjäger Ersatz Regiment 137.

Photographs

(Above) Mountain troops manning a 2cm Flak 30 automatic light anti-aircraft cannon in the ground role. Its light weight of 1698lbs (770kg), and high explosive tracer ammunition fed by 20-round magazines, made it useful in difficult terrain, and its practical rate of fire was 120 rounds per minute. One drawback was the original Linearvisier 21 sight, which required two men – a gun-layer for bearing and elevation, and a range-taker. The crew was five men plus the detachment commander; this crew wear the reversible snow camouflage anorak and trousers, with steel helmets.

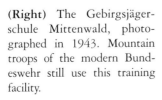

(Right) The Gebirgsjäger-schule Mittenwald, photo-graphed in 1943. Mountain troops of the modern Bund-eswehr still use this training facility.

(**Above**) Generaloberst Eduard Dietl (1890–1944), left, with the chief of staff of his 20th Mountain Army, GenLt Hermann Hölter, at Kirkenes in northern Norway in May 1944.

(**Right**) GenLt Dietl on 26 May 1940 at his headquarters in Bjørnfjell outside Narvik (*see* also page 81). He wears his characteristic uniform: *Bergmütze,* service tunic (with the *Heeresbergführer Abzeichen* of a former qualified mountain leader on the right pocket), old Reichswehr mountain breeches with general's red stripes, long puttees and mountain boots. With him is 3. Gebirgs Division's Catholic chaplain, Dr Josef Maurer – note the Christian cross on his cap and the absence of shoulder boards.

Eduard Dietl was a Bavarian officer who had been wounded four times during World War I. He fought with Freikorps von Epp against the 'Bavarian Red Army' in the streets of Munich in May 1919, and joined the Nazy Party in 1920. He served in the Reichswehr's Infanterie Regiment 19, and in the late 1920s Major Dietl commanded its III (Gebirgsjäger) Bataillon. Between January 1933 and April 1938 he rose from lieutenant-colonel to major-general, in successive command of IR 19, GJR 99, and the new 3. Gebirgs Division. In September 1939 he led his division into Poland, capturing the Dukla Pass in the Carpathians; but it was his defence of Narvik in April-May 1940 that made him a household name in Germany. That battle earned him the first award to a soldier of the newly instituted Oakleaves to the Knight's Cross, on 19 July 1940; he was promoted full general and given command of the Norway Mountain Corps, based in the far north of that country. This corps had evolved into 20. Gebirgs Armee by the time of the invasion of the USSR in June 1941. Early in Operation 'Barbarossa' this army – including XIX Gebirgs Korps, with 2. and 3. Gebirgs Divisionen – struck eastwards across a narrow neck of friendly Finland and into Soviet territory in a dash for the vital arctic port of Murmansk. This offensive failed, and Dietl's army withdrew to defensive positions on the Litsa river in Finland. He was appointed commander of German forces in Lapland in January 1942, and promoted colonel-general that June. The war in this backwater of the Russian

Front degenerated into see-saw attritional fighting under miserable conditions. On 23 June 1944, worried – correctly – that Finland was about to agree separate peace terms with Stalin, Hitler summoned Dietl back to the Führer's mountain retreat in the Obersalzburg for discussions. The general's aircraft crashed in the mountains, killing all on board.

(Top) An example of the horrendous conditions faced by the men and animals who had to shoulder the burden of keeping the Mountain Troops supplied in the front lines. This pony and its handler have been brought to an exhausted halt in a tilted morass of sloppy mud.

(Above) In immaculate contrast, an Obergefreiter of Gebirgsjäger wearing the M36 service uniform. Note the nicest touch – that he has a real edelweiss flower tucked behind the metal insignia on the side of his Bergmütze.

(Above) The short peak of the Bergmütze shows particularly well in this shot of two mountain soldiers examining the broken tip of a ski during training. Judging from the liberal coating of snow, it was the man on the right who took this fall.

Remembrance cards

Like millions of soldiers of many countries, the Gebirgsjäger fought and died on many fronts, far from home and family. In these last pages we remind readers that regardless of nationality, religion or beliefs, all these young men were fellow human beings whose memory should be respected. An old German proverb says: *'A great war leaves the country with three armies – an army of cripples, an army of mourners, and an army of thieves'.*

Stabsfeldwebel Hans Kahr of GJR 98 fell in his 31st year, at Timoshevka in the Ukraine in late September 1941. He died on the third day of 1. Gebirgs Division's battle for a massive anti-tank ditch, a battle not won for another twelve days.

†

Zum Andenken
an

Ing. Hans Blaßnigg

Gefreiter in einem Geb.-Jäg.-Regt.,
gefallen am 2. Mai 1940
bei Ankenes, Narvik (Norwegen).

†

Hansl gab sein Leben im Glauben
an Deutschland. Sein Leib ruht in
fremder Erde, doch sein Geist lebt
in allen weiter, die ihn gekannt
haben.

Er opferte sein Blut.
Mit dem Heldentod hat er seine
Sendung vollbracht!
Im Gebet
sehen wir seine Vollendung.

(**Left**) Young Gefreiter Hans Blaßnigg was an early casualty, who fell in the middle of the battle for Narvik on 2 May 1940.

(**Right**) Feldwebel Anderl Rehrl was 27 years old, a qualified mountain leader, a holder of the Iron Cross 2nd Class and the Wound Badge, and already a veteran of Poland, Greece and the Eastern Front when he fell in Russia on 13 January 1942.

Zur Erinnerung im Gebete
an unsern lieben Sohn und Bruder

Anderl Rehrl
Feldwebel und Heeresbergführer
in einem Gebirgsjägerregiment

Teilnehmer an den Feldzügen Polen, Griechenland
und Sowjetrußland.
Träger des E.K. II und des Verwundeten-Abzeichens,

welcher am 13. Januar 1942 bei den
schweren Kämpfen im Osten im Alter
von 27 Jahren in treuer, soldatischer
Pflichterfüllung sein junges Leben für
seine geliebte Bergheimat gab.

Ich weiß, ihr werdet bitter weinen,
Daß ich so ferne sank ins Grab
Wo nur die stillen Sterne scheinen
In meine dunkle Gruft hinab.
Doch einmal kommt der Tod zu Allen;
Und bricht der Liebe zartes Band,
Wo wär ich herrlicher gefallen,
Als kämpfend treu fürs Vaterland.
Mein früher Tod, mein großes Glück,
Drum meine Lieben weinet nicht
Ich lebe noch und liebe Euch
In Gottes schönem Himmelreich.

Ehre seinem Andenken!

Wiedemannsche Buchdruckerei Bad Reichenhall

Unsterblich ist,
wer für die Heimat fällt!

Frommes Andenken im Gebete
an unseren unvergeßlichen
Sohn und Bruder

Jakob Rieder
Gefr. in einem Geb.-Jäg.-Btl.
in Afrika
Schlosser von Ruhpolding

welcher am 4. Juni 1942 im Alter v.
21½ Jahren in Afrika bei einem
Bombenangriff den Heldentod erlitt

Die Pflicht rief mich zum Krieg hinaus.
Mit Gott ging ich vom Elternhaus.
Im fernen Land, in heißer Schlacht
Da hab ich oft an Euch gedacht
Und freute mich auf's Wiederseh'n,
Wenn Krieg und Sturm zu Ende geh'n.
Doch anders hat's der Herr gewollt
Und hat von hier mich abgeholt.
Weiß nichts von Krieg und Erdenleid
Und bin von jeder Sorg befreit.
Nun ruh' in fremder Erd' ich aus
Und bin in Gottes Vaterhaus.
Drum meine Lieben, denkt stets d'ran,
Was Gott tut, das ist wohlgetan.

(**Left**) Gefreiter Jakob Rieder was a 21-year old Gebirgsjäger serving with the Afrikakorps. He was killed along with seven comrades during a British bomber attack on the Luftwaffe airstrip at Tmimi in Libya on 4 June 1942. They were all members of 2. Kompanie, Sonderverband (special unit) 288, which was a Gebirgsjäger Kompanie.

Wer im Herzen seiner Lieben lebt,
der ist nicht tot, der ist nur fern.

Select bibliography

Ailsby, Christopher, *Combat Medals of the Third Reich*, Patrick Stephens Ltd (Northamptonshire, UK, 1987)

Angolia, John R. & Schlicht, Adolf, *Uniforms & Traditions of the German Army*, 3 vols., R. James Bender Publishing Co (San Jose CA, USA, 1984)

Buchner, Alex, *Der Bergkrieg im Kaukasus*, Podzun-Pallas-Verlag (Friedberg, Germany, 1977)

Diebel, Helmut, *Kameraden Unterm Edelweiss* (Nuremberg, Germany, 1988)

Konrad, R, *Kampf um den Kaukasus,* Copress-Verlag (Munich, Germany, c.1966)

Krawczyk, Wade, *German Army Uniforms of World War II in Colour Photographs*, Windrow & Greene Ltd (London, UK, 1995)

Lucas, James, *Hitler's Mountain Troops*, Arms & Armour Press (London, UK, 1992)

Manz, Hugo, *Bewaffnete Alpenheimat* (Innsbruck, Austria, 1941)

Mitcham, Samuel W., *Hitler's Legions: German Army Order of Battle, World War II* (Leo Cooper/Secker & Warburg, London, UK, 1985)

Quarrie, Bruce, *German Mountain Troops*, Patrick Stephens Ltd (Cambridge, UK, 1980)

Seidel, Max, *Wir tragen stolz das Edelweiß,* Christian Belser Verlagsbuchhandlung (Stuttgart, Germany, 1941)

Tietz, Ulrich, &. Hugo Manz, *Gebirgsjäger in Griechenland und auf Kreta,* Die Wehrmaclat (Berlin, 1942)

Wegmann, Günter, *Die Ritterkreuzträger der Gebirgsjäger,* 2 vols., Biblio Verlag (Osnabrück, Germany, 1994)

Westarp, E.-J.Graf v, *Taschenkalender für Offiziere des Heeres,* Alfred Waberg Verlag (Pommern, Germany, 1943)

Williamson, Gordon, *German Mountain & Ski Troops 1939–45,* Elite 63 (Osprey Publishing, London, UK, 1996)